STRATEGIES
FOR TEACHING
K–4 General Music

MENC wishes to thank
Carolynn A. Lindeman for developing and coordinating this series;
Sandra L. Stauffer and *Jennifer Davidson*
for selecting, writing, and editing the strategies for this book;
and the following teachers for submitting strategies:

Kristin Anderson
Ruth Argabright
Vicki Armour
Carol A. Belmain
Elaine Bernstorf
Patricia Bourne
Patrice Bove
Chelcy Bowles
Dick Bozung
Dina Breaux
Catherine Brodie
Beverly Brook
Ann Burbridge
J. Bryan Burton
Scott Chappell
Eileen Curry
Jo-Ann L. Decker-St. Pierre
Miriam DeLap
Sandra Denmead
Sarah Donahue
Ed Duling
Kay Edwards
Darla Eshelman
Renee Forrest

Martha Giles
Debra G. Gordon
Jana Gutenson
Patricia Hackett
Jean I. Hamann
Darla S. Hanley
Lois N. Harrison
Juliette A. Hawk
Danette Henry
Carol Hillman
Julia Hollenberg
Catherine Jarjisian
Kirk Kassner
Ellen Kaufmann
Tatia Key
Gloria J. Kiester
Helen J. Krehbiel-Reed
Kay H. Logan
Lori Lyford
Peggy McBride
Cindy McCaskill
Pamela S. Moore
Kathleen Moran
Steve Motenko

Kaycee Muffuletta
Dolores Nicholson
Kathleen Marie Nock
Charlene D. Norris
Emma R. Oberheuser
Louise Patrick
Marcia Peteranetz
Brian Querry
Shelley Sasser
Dorothy M. Sheldon
Marcelyn Smale
Stephanie Stickford
Robyn Swanson
Judith Teicher-Boateng
Valerie Vander Mark
Mary Lou Van Rysselberghe
Roberta Volkmann
Stuart Watts
Sherrie Welles
Mary Wick
Jackie Wiggins
Tom Wine
LeAnn Wolf

STRATEGIES FOR TEACHING

K–4 General Music

Compiled and edited by
Sandra L. Stauffer and Jennifer Davidson

MUSIC EDUCATORS NATIONAL CONFERENCE

YOUR KEY TO IMPLEMENTING THE NATIONAL STANDARDS FOR MUSIC EDUCATION

MENC MENC
MENC MENC

CONTENTS

PREFACE

The Music Educators National Conference (MENC) created the *Strategies for Teaching* series to help preservice and in-service music educators implement the K–12 National Standards for Music Education and the MENC Prekindergarten Standards. To address the many components of the school music curriculum, each book in the series focuses on a specific curricular area and a particular level. The result is eleven books spanning the K–12 areas of band, chorus, general music, strings/orchestra, guitar, keyboard, and specialized ensembles. A prekindergarten book and a guide for college music methods classes complete the series.

The purpose of the series is to seize the opportunity presented by the landmark education legislation of 1994. With the passage of the Goals 2000: Educate America Act, the arts were established for the first time in our country's history as a core, challenging subject in which all students need to demonstrate competence. Voluntary academic standards were called for in all nine of the identified core subjects—standards specifying what students need to know and be able to do when they exit grades 4, 8, and 12.

In music, content and achievement standards were drafted by an MENC task force. They were examined and commented on by music teachers across the country, and the task force reviewed their comments and refined the standards. While all students in grades K–8 are expected to meet the achievement standards specified for those levels, two levels of achievement—proficient and advanced—are designated for students in grades 9–12. Students who elect music courses for one to two years beyond grade 8 are expected to perform at the proficient level. Students who elect music courses for three to four years beyond grade 8 are expected to perform at the advanced level.

The music standards, together with the dance, theatre, and visual arts standards, were presented in final form—*National Standards for Arts Education*—to the U.S. Secretary of Education in March 1994. Recognizing the importance of early childhood education, MENC went beyond the K–12 standards and established content and achievement standards for the prekindergarten level as well, which are included in MENC's *The School Music Program: A New Vision.*

Now the challenge at hand is to implement the standards at the state and local levels. Implementation may require schools to expand the resources necessary to achieve the standards as specified in MENC's *Opportunity-to-Learn Standards for Music Instruction: Grades PreK–12.* Teachers will need to examine their curricula to determine if they lead to achievement of the standards. For many, the standards reflect exactly what has always been included in the school music curriculum—they represent best practice. For others, the standards may call for some curricular expansion.

To assist in the implementation process, this series offers teaching strategies illustrating how the music standards can be put into action in the music classroom. The strategies themselves do not suggest a curriculum. That, of course, is the responsibility of school districts and individual teachers. The strategies, however, are designed to help in curriculum development, lesson planning, and assessment of music learning.

The teaching strategies are based on the content and achievement standards specified in the *National Standards for Arts Education* (K–12) and *The School Music Program: A New Vision* (PreK–12). Although the strategies, like the standards, are designed primarily for four-year-olds, fourth graders, eighth graders, and high school seniors, many may be developmentally appropriate for students in other grades. Each strategy, a lesson appropriate for a portion of a class session or a complete class session, includes an objective (a clear statement of what the student will be able to do), a list of necessary materials, a description of what prior student learning and experiences are expected, a set of procedures, and the indicators of success. A follow-up section identifies ways learning may be expanded.

The *Guide for Music Methods Classes* contains strategies appropriate for preservice instructional settings in choral, instrumental, and general music methods classes. The teaching strategies in this guide relate to the other books in the series and reflect a variety of teaching/learning styles.

Bringing a series of thirteen books from vision to reality in a little over a year's time required tremendous commitment from many, many music educators—not to mention the tireless help of the MENC publications staff. Literally hundreds of music teachers across the country answered the call to participate in this project, the largest such participation in an MENC publishing endeavor. The contributions of these teachers and the books' editors are proudly presented in the various publications.

—*Carolynn A. Lindeman*
Series Editor

Carolynn A. Lindeman, professor of music at San Francisco State University, served on the MENC task force that developed the music education standards. She is the author of three college textbooks (The Musical Classroom, PianoLab, *and* MusicLab) *and numerous articles.*

INTRODUCTION

Children arrive in elementary school with ears, minds, and hearts full of music from their homes, communities, and the media. Music of diverse styles, genres, and cultures is already woven into the knowledge and experience of students in kindergarten through grade four. During these years, children continue to learn about music through their experiences both in school and outside of school.

Children in the early grades are active learners who make music by singing and playing instruments. When they listen to music, they respond naturally by moving, singing, or playing along. They create their own tunes, rhythms, and songs spontaneously and within contexts arranged for them. As their cognitive abilities develop, children learn to read notation and use music vocabulary to talk about the music they hear. Elementary school music programs contribute to the musical growth of children by nurturing their musical interests and abilities, broadening their musical horizons, and enriching their knowledge about music.

The National Standards for Music Education reflect a broad-based national consensus about what students should know and be able to do in music. The standards for grades K–4 are written as exit standards for fourth-grade students. They state what fourth-grade children should be able to achieve in music by the end of the school year, given comprehensive music instruction in the elementary grades. (See MENC's *Opportunity-to-Learn Standards for Music Instruction: Grades PreK–12* for further information about time and resources required to support comprehensive music instruction in the elementary grades.)

Because the K–4 standards are written as exit standards for grade four, the lessons that appear on the following pages target fourth-grade students. These sample lessons are presented in the same order as the content and achievement standards appear in the *National Standards for Arts Education*. They are not arranged sequentially for successive grades or classes, nor do they represent a curriculum for fourth-grade music.

One lesson is presented for each of the grade four achievement standards statements. Prior experiences and knowledge required for success appear at the beginning of each lesson. When students complete the lesson successfully, they have met, either in whole or in part, that particular achievement standard for grade four. Each lesson represents, however, only one of many ways in which the achievement standard may be met.

While these lessons may be used as written, all of them can and should be adapted to meet local needs and circumstances. Some may be completed during a single class period; others may be used over several class meetings, depending on time restrictions and the needs and abilities of students. A lesson component may evolve into an extended activity. Different singing and listening repertoire may be substituted in many of the lessons and teaching suggestions presented.

Children learn most about music when the classroom environment is rich with musical examples and affords both multiple and varied opportunities to engage in music making. Although each lesson presented in the following pages focuses on one achievement standard, the depth and breadth of learning often exceeds the standard indicated at the top of the page. A composition lesson (Content Standard 4), for example, may include reading or writing music notation (Content Standard 5), playing instruments (Content Standard 2), and students' evaluation of their own work (Content Standard 7).

The lessons in this book represent the thinking and practice of general music teachers across the United States. Their strategies for sharing music with children are as varied as the schools in which they teach and the children they serve. We thank them for sharing their ideas and strategies with other general music educators by contributing to this document, and we salute their creativity and dedication to the musical growth of children everywhere.

STRATEGIES

STANDARD 1A

Singing, alone and with others, a varied repertoire of music: Students sing independently, on pitch and in rhythm, with appropriate timbre, diction, and posture, and maintain a steady tempo.

Objective

- Students will demonstrate appropriate singing skills while performing a familiar song as a class and with a small group of four or five peers.

Materials

- Class list of familiar songs
- Chalkboard or overhead projector and blank transparency

Prior Knowledge and Experiences

- Students have listed songs they can sing as a class in their music journals or on a chart.
- Students have worked on developing specific singing skills (such as diction and posture) in previous lessons.

Procedures

1. Invite students to choose a familiar song from the class list posted in the room or written in their journals. Ask students to list hints and reminders for using good singing posture. List their suggestions on a transparency or the chalkboard. As the class sings the song, have students check their own posture and then the posture of a partner.

2. Ask students to suggest ways in which they might improve the class performance of the song. Record student suggestions and check for understanding among class members. Choose two of the students' suggestions (for example, "We were singing too fast" or "We need to pronounce all the words clearly") as the focus points for the next step.

3. Before the class sings the song again, appoint two or more students as "Checkers," who listen as the class sings the song again. Have the students perform the song a second time, paying attention to the two suggestions for improvement chosen previously. Invite the "Checkers" to report their observations after the class performance.

4. Select another song from the class list. Divide the class into cooperative groups of four or five. Ask each group to practice the song together and to coach each other on appropriate singing skills. These directions may be posted or shown on an overhead transparency for quick reference. You may also wish to give each group a resonator bell or some other instrument with which to give themselves a starting pitch.

5. After a specified practice time, invite small groups to perform for each other or for the class. After all groups have sung, allow each group to assess its own performance. If students are keeping journals, encourage them to write an assessment of their own and the group's singing ability. (*Note: Having students perform in small groups also allows the teacher greater opportunity to assess each individual's singing ability.*)

Indicators of Success

- Both the class and small groups of students perform their songs with appropriate singing skills.

- Student verbal and/or written self-assessments of their singing ability reflect knowledge of singing skills, such as pitch, rhythm, posture, timbre, diction, and tempo.

Follow-up

- On another day, follow the same procedures using a call-and-response song. Have individuals sing the call and small groups of students or the rest of the class sing the response. Have each student select one or more specific singing skills (for example, pitch and posture) as the focus for self-assessment.

STANDARD 1B

Singing, alone and with others, a varied repertoire of music: Students sing expressively, with appropriate dynamics, phrasing, and interpretation.

Objective

- Students will identify dynamic markings and will apply their knowledge of dynamics when performing a familiar song in unison and in canon.

Materials

- A familiar canon, such as "The Ghost of John," in *Share the Music,* Grade 4 (New York: Macmillan/ McGraw-Hill, 1995); *Music and You,* Grade 5 (New York: Macmillan/McGraw-Hill, 1991); or *World of Music,* Grade 3, Parsippany, NJ: Silver Burdett Ginn, 1991)

- Overhead projector and transparency or chart of the song

- Cards with the dynamic symbols *pp, p, mp, mf, f, ff,* crescendo, decrescendo (one symbol per card)

- Audiocassette recorder with microphone and blank tape

Prior Knowledge and Experiences

- Students have prior experience singing rounds and canons.

Procedures

1. Sing a greeting to the students and invite them to echo (for example, "Welcome to music class," sung using *sol-mi-la-sol-sol-mi*). Show students a card with a dynamic marking written on it. Ask the students to identify the marking by its Italian name and English definition; then have them sing the greeting using that dynamic. Continue this procedure to review other dynamic markings. Remind students that even loud singing must sound musical.

2. Review "The Ghost of John" and have students sing the song in unison, as they remember it from the last class session. Tape record the students' performance of the song for use later in the lesson.

3. Ask students to examine the notation of the song in their student texts. Identify any dynamic markings already present in the music, and have the students sing the song again, observing the marks they have identified.

4. Show the students a copy of the music, via chart or overhead transparency, with no dynamic markings. Tell the students that they may experiment with the dynamics to create an interpretation they like. Invite them to suggest alternatives by having different students conduct (hands together = soft; hands apart moving vertically = loud) while the class sings.

5. Ask students to arrive at a class decision about the dynamics they will use while singing "The Ghost of John." Encourage students to give supporting reasons for their choices and suggestions. Ask students to record the decisions of the class by writing the appropriate markings at the point of use on the overhead transparency or chart of the song.

6. Tape record a class performance of "The Ghost of John" that uses the dynamics students have suggested. Have students listen to their performance and tell a partner whether the performance reflected the dynamics decided upon by the class.

7. Ask students to listen to and compare their performances of "The Ghost of John" from the beginning of class and after adding the dynamics they have determined. Have students describe how their interpretation of the dynamics improved their performance of the song.

- Students recognize and can define the dynamic symbols *pp, p, mp, mf, f, ff,* crescendo, and decrescendo.

- Students have learned the melody of "The Ghost of John" during the previous class and have sung the song in unison.

Indicators of Success

- Students verbally identify dynamic markings and sing "The Ghost of John" with the dynamic interpretation prepared by the class.

- Students can describe how the use of dynamics has improved their performance of the song.

Follow-up

- During the next class session, review the dynamic interpretation of "The Ghost of John" created by the class. Have the students sing the song in canon, with each group following the dynamics.

- On another day, have students add instrumental ostinatos to accompany the song and apply various dynamic markings to them.

STANDARD 1C

Singing, alone and with others, a varied repertoire of music: Students sing from memory a varied repertoire of songs representing genres and styles from diverse cultures.

Objective

- Students will be able to sing "Sorida," a song from the Shona people of Zimbabwe, Africa, following aural listening and rote teaching.

Materials

- "Sorida," in *Let Your Voice Be Heard* by Abraham Kobena Adzinyah, Dumisani Maraire, and Judith Cook Tucker (Danbury, CT: World Music Press, 1986), with accompanying recording
- Audio-playback equipment

Prior Knowledge and Experiences

- Students can recognize and identify repeated phrases in songs.
- Students have basic knowledge of the lifeways of various African peoples.

Procedures

1. After the class enters the room and is seated on the floor, ask students to listen to a recording of "Sorida" and to identify repeated musical ideas and repeated words.

2. After the students have listened to the song, question them about what they heard in the song (three pitches, short phrases, an increase in tempo as the song progressed).

3. Tell students about the context of "Sorida," including where the Shona people live in Africa, the oral tradition of learning songs, the meaning of the text, and the structure of the song. Teach each phrase of "Sorida" by rote, clarifying lyrics for students who encounter difficulty in hearing new words.

4. Have the class perform the entire song, gradually accelerating the tempo in imitation of the recording.

5. At the close of the lesson, have students tell a partner something they have learned about the song "Sorida" and about the Shona people.

Indicators of Success

- Students will sing "Sorida" correctly, following rote instruction.
- Students will recall contextual and structural information, such as the location and traditions of the Shona people, the meaning of the text, the number of pitches in the song, and the repeated phrases in the song "Sorida."

Follow-up

- Add the game activity that accompanies this song.
- On another day, compare "Sorida" to other African singing games and singing games from other cultures.

STANDARD 1D

Singing, alone and with others, a varied repertoire of music:
Students sing ostinatos, partner songs, and rounds.

Objective

- Students will successfully sing one melody while classmates sing a different melody, an ostinato, or the same melody in canon.

Materials

- Any song that can be performed in a round; any song with an ostinato; any two partner songs
- Audiocassette recorder with microphone and blank tape (optional)

Prior Knowledge and Experiences

- Students can successfully sing the songs and ostinatos used in the lesson.
- Students sing the song or songs selected with appropriate vocal technique.

Procedures

1. Ask students to sing a familiar song that can later be performed as a round or to which an ostinato or partner song can be added. While they sing, have students focus on vocal technique. Then guide students through a critique of their performance.

2. Invite students to sing the song again while you sing an ostinato or partner song or the second part of the round, depending on the song you have selected. If you have chosen a round, have students begin first and you enter second. Remind students to focus on their melody, not yours. Ask students to tap the beat quietly to help secure the tempo as needed.

3. When students can successfully sing their part in Step 2, ask for two or three volunteers to help you sing your part. Repeat the performance, with the class singing the song while you and student volunteers sing the harmony part.

4. Repeat Step 3, adding two more volunteers to the smaller group. As the class gains confidence, continue to repeat the song with the harmony part and add volunteers to the small group until the class is evenly divided. Adjust the groupings if necessary to create a balance.

5. To check for security of parts and to provide an additional listening experience, ask each half of the class to sing the song and then its partner or ostinato (if using a round, just sing the song through). Next, have each half of the class sing the song while you sing the harmony part and the other half of the class listens. Ask each half of the class to critique its own performance as well as that of the other group.

6. Finally, ask the students to sing again in counterpoint with each other—one half of the class on the song and the other half on the harmony part. Remind students that the challenge is not to outsing the other group, but to produce a pleasing musical sound by collaboration. Ask the students to tap the beat quietly to secure the tempo as needed. If an audiocassette recorder with microphone is available, record the students' two-part singing. Then have them listen to the recording and critique their performance.

Indicators of Success

■ Students sing in two parts.

■ Students demonstrate appropriate vocal technique and collaborative skills in producing appealing two-part music.

Follow-up

■ Have students sing other songs to which an ostinato (sung) or partner song can be added, or have them sing other songs that can be performed in canon.

■ When students can sing in two parts securely and comfortably, introduce three-part singing using similar techniques.

STANDARD 1E

Singing, alone and with others, a varied repertoire of music: Students sing in groups, blending vocal timbres, matching dynamic levels, and responding to the cues of a conductor.

Objective

- Students will perform "The Birch Tree" in unison while attending and responding to vocal blending, dynamic levels, and conductor cues.

Materials

- "The Birch Tree," in *The Music Connection,* Grade 4 (Parsippany, NJ: Silver Burdett Ginn, 1995); *Music and You,* Grade 7 (New York: Macmillan/McGraw-Hill, 1991); or *World of Music,* Grade 4 (Parsippany, NJ: Silver Burdett Ginn, 1991)

Prior Knowledge and Experiences

- Students have sung "The Birch Tree" in a class choir format with the teacher as conductor.

- Students know that "The Birch Tree" is a Russian folk song.

- Prior singing experiences have included attention to vocal blending.

Procedures

1. Review the song "The Birch Tree" while you act as conductor. Ask students to listen to each other.

2. After singing "The Birch Tree," ask students to tell what they think vocal blending is and why it is important for good ensemble singing. Using "The Birch Tree," have small groups of students demonstrate good and poor examples of vocal blending to the class. For example, ask four students to sing the song, with two students singing *piano* and two singing *forte.* After listening to a few examples, ask students to describe how dynamics contribute to vocal blending.

3. Demonstrate the conducting gestures for increasing and decreasing dynamic levels. Have students sing "The Birch Tree" while you lead the dynamic interpretation. Ask students to describe why it is important for *all* singers to follow dynamics levels indicated by the conductor.

4. Have student conductors lead the song using appropriate gestures for dynamics. Ask students in the ensemble and student conductors to describe what they heard at the end of each performance.

5. Rehearse "The Birch Tree" with you acting as the conductor, attending to blending and dynamics. Then have students discuss with a partner and/or write in their music journals about the ways in which vocal blend, dynamics and conductor cues/gestures are related to each other and to a musical performance of a song.

Indicators of Success

- Students sing with blended voices and follow conductor cues for dynamics while performing "The Birch Tree."

- Students can describe the relationship of dynamics and vocal blending.

Follow-up

- During the next class, extend blend and dynamics to a performance of "The Birch Tree" in canon.

- Encourage different students to conduct each half of the ensemble when singing in canon.

- Tape record the performance and ask students to evaluate their singing.

STANDARD 2A

Performing on instruments, alone and with others, a varied repertoire of music: Students perform on pitch, in rhythm, with appropriate dynamics and timbre, and maintain a steady tempo.

Objective

- Students will play a two-note countermelody on recorders to the refrain of "Somebody's Knockin' at Your Door."

Materials

- Recorders
- "Somebody's Knockin' at Your Door" (written in or transposed to the key of D), in *The Music Connection,* Grade 4 (Parsippany, NJ: Silver Burdett Ginn, 1995); *Music and You,* Grade 4 (New York: Macmillan/McGraw-Hill, 1991); or *World of Music,* Grade 4 (Parsippany, NJ: Silver Burdett Ginn, 1991)
- Overhead projector and transparency or chart with two-note countermelody (see the example)

Prior Knowledge and Experiences

- Students can sing "Somebody's Knockin' at Your Door."
- Students have played the recorder and know how to play the notes A and B.
- Students can read the rhythms of the countermelody.

Procedures

1. Invite the students to sing the refrain of "Somebody's Knockin' at Your Door." Tell students that they will be learning a harmony part on recorders to accompany the refrain of the song.

2. Show students the following countermelody on a chart or overhead transparency. Have students read, speak, and tap the rhythm of the countermelody and then identify the pitches. Have the students tap the rhythm of the countermelody while you sing the refrain of "Somebody's Knockin' at Your Door." Invite students to both tap the countermelody and sing the song.

3. Distribute recorders. Ask students to demonstrate correct playing position and fingerings for the notes A and B. Echo rhythm patterns using the notes A and B. Ask the students for suggestions about how to improve the tone quality of their playing. Encourage them to implement these suggestions as you continue the echoes.

4. Return to the countermelody for "Somebody's Knockin' at Your Door." Have students finger the notes and sing the pitches as a final rehearsal before playing.

5. Have students play the countermelody. Ask them to assess their tone quality before performing it again. When the students play a second time, sing the melody of "Somebody's Knockin' at Your Door" with them. Repeat, with some students singing the melody as the remainder of the class plays.

6. Divide the class into groups of three. Allow students practice time during which two students in the group play the countermelody and one checks for good tone and accurate rhythm and pitches. Students switch roles until all have had the opportunity to check their peers.

7. When the class reassembles, divide the group in half. Have each half of the class play the countermelody while the other half listens and checks for accurate rhythm and good tone. Then invite half the class to sing the song while the other half plays the countermelody.

Indicators of Success

- Students play the countermelody with correct pitches and rhythms.
- Students demonstrate appropriate playing position and fingerings for the notes of the countermelody.

Follow-up

- Play other songs with countermelodies, extending the number of pitches and complexity of rhythms used.
- Play melodies on the recorder using the same pitches and rhythms.

STANDARD 2B

Performing on instruments, alone and with others, a varied repertoire of music: Students perform easy rhythmic, melodic, and chordal patterns accurately and independently on rhythmic, melodic, and harmonic classroom instruments.

Objective

- Students will accompany "Happiness Runs" using a melodic pattern played on resonator bells and a harmonic pattern played on Autoharps/ChromAharps.

Materials

- "Happiness Runs," in *The Music Connection,* Grade 4 (Parsippany: NJ: Silver Burdett Ginn, 1995) and accompanying CD
- CD player
- Three or four chorded zithers (such as Autoharps or ChromAharps)
- Resonator bells (melody bells or Orff instruments may be substituted for resonator bells)

Prior Knowledge and Experiences

- Students have learned "Happiness Runs" and can sing it well independently prior to adding the accompaniment in this lesson.
- Students have experience accompanying songs using various classroom instruments.

Procedures

1. Have the students sing "Happiness Runs" with the recorded accompaniment or one provided by the teacher. Ask them to sing the song a second time, and have them pat half-note beats as they sing.

2. Show students a chord chart (F-C-G⁷-C), or have them identify the chord symbols in the printed music and find the repeated pattern. Ask students, while working in pairs, to play the chord pattern on Autoharps/ChromAharps, with one student as the player and the other as the coach. After the students have practiced the pattern, have each pair play as the class sings the song. At the end of the song, coaches and players exchange roles.

3. Introduce an ostinato to be played on resonator bells (F-E-D-C, descending) by showing the following movement pattern: pat right-left-right (crossover)-left (to the left), moving right to left across laps or on the floor. Have students move according to the pattern as they sing "Happiness Runs." Sing the pitches F-E-D-C while moving to the pattern, then transfer to the bells. Have students work in player-coach pairs as they did for the aforementioned Autoharp/ChromAharp part.

4. Invite students to sing "Happiness Runs" and play the melodic and harmonic patterns they have learned to accompany the song. Continue to rotate players and coaches as the class repeats the song.

5. At the conclusion of the class, direct students to tell a partner one way in which they added harmony to the song and one helpful hint for performing the accompaniment patterns they learned correctly.

Indicators of Success

- Students accurately perform patterns on the Autoharp/ChromAharp and resonator bells to accompany the song.
- Students give verbal suggestions regarding how to improve or sustain the accuracy of their performance.
- Students describe how the harmony is created in this activity.

Follow-up

- On another day, have students perform additional patterns on unpitched percussion instruments, such as bass notes for the chords on a bass xylophone.

- Have students use instrumental patterns to accompany other songs.

- Invite students to write and perform their own instrumental patterns to create instrumental compositions or to add accompaniments to familiar songs.

STANDARD 2C

Performing on instruments, alone and with others, a varied repertoire of music: Students perform expressively a varied repertoire of music representing diverse genres and styles.

Objectives

- Students will accompany "Que llueva!" with baritone ukuleles.

- Students will perform the melody of the song on alto xylophones or recorders.

Materials

- "Que llueva!" (written in or transposed to the key of C), in *The Music Connection,* Grade 2 (Parsippany, NJ: Silver Burdett Ginn, 1995); or *Share the Music,* Grade 3 (New York: Macmillan/ McGraw-Hill, 1995)

- Baritone ukuleles

- Audiocassette recorder with microphone and blank tape

Prior Knowledge and Experiences

- Students have sung "Que llueva!" in Spanish and have played the game that accompanies the song.

- Students are learning to play ukuleles and have already learned the two chords (C and G) required to accompany "Que llueva!" but have not played the song prior to this lesson.

- Students can identify chord symbols in printed music.

Procedures

1. Have the students review the song "Que llueva!" and play the singing game that accompanies the song.

2. Distribute baritone ukuleles. (Students may work in player-coach pairs and switch roles during the lesson.) Review the C and G chords. To build facility in changing chords, initiate the following four-beat pattern: students strum on beats 1 and 2 and then change fingers to the next chord on beats 3 and 4. Next, students strum on 1-2-3 and change on 4. Finally, students strum on all beats, changing chords every four.

3. Direct students to look at "Que llueva!" in their texts. Ask them to identify the chord symbols and determine which chords are used to accompany the song. Have the students finger the chord changes as they follow the music while you play the chords on a baritone ukulele. Then invite the students to play the accompaniment with you.

4. Using the *think-pair-share* format (a cooperative learning strategy in which individual students think about the answer to a question or problem, discuss the answer with a partner, and then share their answers with the class), ask students to experiment with different kinds of strumming patterns they might use to accompany the song. After students experiment individually, encourage partners to select a pattern they think best fits the style of the song.

5. Ask pairs of students to share the strumming patterns they have selected with the class. Have the class try different suggestions as they accompany the song.

6. Using the *think-pair-share* format again, ask students to determine which strumming pattern should be performed for a class recording of the song and why. As the students share their preferences for strumming patterns with the class, encourage them to give supporting reasons for selecting the patterns they have chosen.

7. Have the students perform the song with ukulele accompaniment. Tape record their performance. Invite the students to listen to the recording and tell their partners one aspect of the performance they liked and one suggestion for improvement. Practice and tape record again as time permits.

Indicators of Success

- Students play the C and G chords to accompany "Que llueva!"
- Students choose appropriate strumming patterns for the song and verbally describe the reasons for their choices.

Follow-up

- On another day, add maracas as an ostinato percussion accompaniment for "Que llueva!"
- Invite students to play the melody of "Que llueva!" on recorders or alto xylophones.
- Extend learning by playing ukulele accompaniments for other Mexican songs in contrasting styles (for example, the dance song "La raspa" or the lullaby "Las estrellitas del cielo"). Allow students to experiment with strumming patterns and/or percussion ostinatos to match the style of each song.

STANDARD 2D

*Performing on instruments, alone and with others, a varied repertoire
of music: Students echo short rhythms and melodic patterns.*

Objective

- Students will echo patterns
  using body percussion and
  unpitched percussion instruments.

Materials

- A short four-phrase or four-
  line poem of your choice
- Unpitched classroom percussion instruments

Prior Knowledge and Experiences

- Students have prior experience echo clapping and performing echoes with other
  body percussion, such as
  snapping, patting, and stamp-
  ing.
- Students have played an array
  of unpitched percussion
  instruments and are familiar
  with basic playing techniques
  (for example, how to hold the
  instruments, where to strike
  to get the best sound).

Procedures

1. Lead the class in body percussion echoes using a variety of movements and rhythms.

2. Introduce the poem you have selected by reciting it in rhythm.
   Have the students learn the poem by rote and then recite it while
   tapping the beat.

3. Clap the rhythm of a phrase from the poem without speaking and
   ask the students to echo. After they clap, ask them to identify the
   words of the poem that match the rhythm. Continue with several
   echoes to assess students' inner hearing and ability to associate
   words with rhythm.

4. Recite the poem together and keep the beat. At the end of the
   poem, invite students to echo four body percussion patterns, each
   four beats long, and then recite the poem again. (The body percussion echoes become an interlude between repetitions of the
   poem.) Continue the process for several repetitions of the poem.
   As they grow more comfortable with the process, choose students
   to lead the echo interludes.

5. Have the students transfer rhythms of the poem to unpitched percussion instruments. Instruments may be assigned to different
   lines, words, or phrases, depending on the poem you have selected. Have students play the percussion instruments with or without
   reciting the poem while continuing teacher-led or student-led
   body percussion echoes between each repetition of the poem, or
   have students continue to recite the poem and perform the interlude echoes on unpitched percussion instruments. The whole class
   may echo the interlude patterns, or patterns may be directed to
   small groups of students playing similar instruments, depending
   on class size and instrument availability.

Indicators of Success

- Students perform rhythm echoes accurately while using body percussion and unpitched percussion instruments.

Follow-up

- Invite students to speak the selected poem in canon for additional variation in this lesson.

- Have students transfer body percussion or unpitched percussion echoes to mallet percussion instruments. Arrange bars of pitched percussion in a pentatonic scale. Students can then echo a rhythm pattern by playing it on a single note of their choice, or by playing any pattern of notes. Specific pitches may be echoed as students gain facility.

STANDARD 2E

Performing on instruments, alone and with others, a varied repertoire of music: Students perform in groups, blending instrumental timbres, matching dynamic levels, and responding to the cues of a conductor.

Objectives

- While working in groups, students will create an accompaniment for "Tzena, Tzena" using at least three instruments.
- Students will determine an appropriate balance and blend of accompaniment parts for "Tzena, Tzena" and then perform their accompaniments for the class.

Materials

- Student texts with the song "Tzena, Tzena," in *The Music Connection,* Grade 5 (Parsippany, NJ: Silver Burdett Ginn, 1995); *Share the Music,* Grade 5 (New York: Macmillan/McGraw-Hill, 1995); or *Music and You,* Grade 6 (New York: Macmillan/McGraw-Hill, 1991)
- Overhead projector and transparency or chart of "Tzena, Tzena"
- Chorded zithers (such as Autoharps or ChromAharps), keyboards, xylophones, glockenspiels, recorders, tambourines, finger cymbals, hand drums, or any other classroom instruments

Procedures

1. Invite the students to sing "Tzena, Tzena" and play the xylophone part they have learned during the previous class. Switch players with every repetition of the song.

2. Sing the song again and ask the students to snap their fingers twice each time a new section of the song begins. Sing the song once more and ask the students to think about how they would identify or label the parts of the song. Ask them for their decisions at the end of the song. (The song has three main sections: ABC.) Have students sing the song again to determine how the three sections are similar and how they are different. Allow them to refer to their student texts as needed. (The melody, rhythm, and most of the words are different. Each section is the same length and uses nearly the same chord/bass pattern.)

3. Divide the class into three groups and assign each group one section of the song. Give the students the following task: (1) Each group must create an accompaniment for its section of the song. (2) The accompaniment should include at least three different instruments. (3) Each group must appoint a conductor to lead it. (4) The group must sing the song and perform the accompaniment for the class. (It may be helpful to post these directions on a chart or overhead transparency for quick reference as the students work in groups.)

4. Before the groups begin their work, ask the class to determine the criteria by which they will be able to assess the performance of their section of the song and accompaniment. For example, the audience must be able to hear all the parts, and the parts must stay together. Give each group any additional information required, such as possible recorder countermelodies.

5. At the end of a given work time, ask each group to sing its section of the song and perform the accompaniment they have created. Have each group assess its own performance using the criteria developed earlier in the lesson, as well as the performances of the other groups.

6. Ask students how the group accompaniments may have to change if the entire class sings instead of the group members only. Invite the class to experiment with the dynamics of each section and the accompanying instrumental parts.

Prior Knowledge and Experiences

- Students have learned "Tzena, Tzena" in a previous class and have played the bass notes of the chords used to accompany the song on xylophones.

- Students have played the recorder, Autoharp/ChromA-harp, and unpitched percussion instruments.

7. Record a class performance of the song with the three instrumental accompaniment groups playing only during the section on which they worked. Have the students listen to the recording and assess their performance using the criteria they developed earlier.

Indicators of Success

- Students create accompaniments appropriate for "Tzena, Tzena."

- In small group performances of sections of "Tzena, Tzena," students balance and blend vocal and instrumental parts.

- Students use dynamics terms correctly when arranging a whole-class performance of the song with accompaniment, and they adjust the balance of parts appropriately.

Follow-up

- Arrange for students to perform for another class or for a parent or community group. Allow students to describe their accompaniment and how they created it.

- During subsequent classes, invite the students to create accompaniments for other songs with which they are familiar.

STANDARD 2F

Performing on instruments, alone and with others, a varied repertoire of music: Students perform independent instrumental parts while other students sing or play contrasting parts.

Objective

- Students will accompany "Turn the Glasses Over" with ostinatos performed on pitched and unpitched percussion instruments.

Materials

- "Turn the Glasses Over," in *120 Singing Games and Dances for Elementary Schools* by Lois Choksy and David Brummitt (Englewood Cliffs, NJ: Prentice-Hall, 1987)
- Ostinato patterns written on cards
- Pitched and unpitched percussion instruments

Prior Knowledge and Experiences

- Students have sung "Turn the Glasses Over" in a previous class and have learned the movement/play party that goes with the song.
- Students have experience accompanying songs using ostinatos.

Procedures

1. Ask students to review "Turn the Glasses Over," first by singing and assessing their singing tone, then by adding the movements they have learned to the song.

2. While seated on the floor, invite the students to move the following pattern: pat-snap-snap-snap.

3. Transfer the body percussion pattern to a bass metallophone, striking *do* and *sol* together (bordun) on the first beat of the pattern and raising hands or resting on beats 2 through 4 as the sound sustains. (Students with less experience may tap the sticks of the mallets together on beats 2 through 4.) Show students the notated pattern on a card, or have a student notate the pattern on a card. Place the card next to the instrument as a reminder for students when they exchange parts and instruments.

4. Sing the song and accompany with the bordun. Select a class evaluator to listen to the performance and tell the group whether the song and accompaniment stayed together.

5. Continue to add other pitched and unpitched ostinatos to the song using a similar process: sing and move the pattern, transfer the pattern to the instrument (sing melodic ostinatos during this step), and then add the pattern to the developing musical texture. Rotate players and class evaluators with each repetition of the song.

6. At the end of the class, have students assess their ability to play the ostinato parts by writing in their journals which part they played and how well they were able to play it. Invite students to make a class list of hints for improving their performance. Refer to the class list in subsequent lessons.

Indicators of Success

- Students perform various accompaniment ostinatos simultaneously while singing "Turn the Glasses Over."

Follow-up

- Listen to recorded examples of music with ostinato accompaniment (e.g., Georges Bizet's "Carillon" from *L'Arlésienne Suite no. 1,* Gustav Holst's "Mars," from *The Planets;* Zoltán Kodály's "The Viennese Musical Clock," from *The Háry János Suite;* Gustav Mahler's Third Movement (A section) from Symphony no. 1, Marin Marais's *The Bells of St. Geneviève;* Carl Orff's "O Fortuna," from *Carmina Burana;* Sergei Prokofiev's "Troika" (A section), from *Lieutenant Kijé Suite;* and Igor Stravinsky's "Berceuse," from *Firebird Suite.*

- Using a different pentatonic song, divide students into three or four groups and allow them to create their own ostinato accompaniments to the song. Have the groups sing and perform their accompaniments for each other.

STANDARD 3A

Improvising melodies, variations, and accompaniments: Students improvise "answers" in the same style to given rhythmic and melodic phrases.

Objective

- Students will improvise rhythm "answers" on timpani or hand drums in response to rhythm "questions" played by a teacher or classmate.

Materials

- Hand drums and/or classroom timpani or roto-toms

Prior Knowledge and Experiences

- Students have experience echoing rhythm patterns of various lengths and in different meters using unpitched percussion and body percussion.

- Students have experience playing hand drums and other drums available in the classroom.

Procedures

1. Initiate a series of body percussion echoes with the students. Tell the students that instead of imitating you exactly, they are going to improvise their own rhythms in question/answer style.

2. Before starting the musical question/answer improvisations, ask students for possible answers to the question, "What did you have for lunch today?" After listening to their answers, give students some additional choices to demonstrate the relationship between questions and answers. For example, "Giraffes are my favorite animal" could be an answer to a question, but not to the question asked. "I had bacon and eggs for breakfast" is closer, but still not an answer to the question asked.

3. Demonstrate the question/answer idea and the relationship between question and answer using rhythms. Clap a possible "question" rhythm and then show students examples of good "answers" (for example, similar rhythms and same length) and not-so-good "answers" (for example, different tempo, a much longer rhythm, or a triple meter answer to a duple meter question). Ask students to describe why they think some of the possible rhythm answers you gave were better than others.

4. Return to the body percussion echoes and invite students to improvise their own answers in response to your questions. Begin with one body sound and simple rhythms; gradually add more sounds and complex rhythms.

5. Invite students to find a partner with whom they will improvise. Have one student clap the question and another clap the answer. After several minutes of practice time, divide the class into two groups and ask each group to line up behind one of two drums.

6. Using a third drum, play a question to the first student in the first line. After the student plays an answer, play a question to the first student in the second line. Have students rotate to the end of the line after they have played, so the question/answer sequence can continue uninterrupted. Have students who are awaiting their turns pat the beat on their thighs during the questions and tap the beat on their shoulders during the answers. This will help students feel the length of patterns as their turn approaches.

7. As students become more comfortable with improvised rhythms, designate one drum as the "question drum" and the other as the "answer drum." Invite the students to line up behind the two drums as before and improvise questions and answers to each other. Students rotate to the end of the opposite line after they have played. While students are waiting for their turn, have them keep a two-beat pattern, such as pat-snap, or pat on thighs and shoulders as in Step 6.

Indicators of Success

- Students improvise new rhythms to given questions rather than imitating what they hear.

- Students' improvised answers are the same length, at the same tempo, and use similar rhythms to given questions.

Follow-up

- Assign students to small groups to continue the question/answer improvisations. Students may select two different instruments on which to perform their improvisations.

- Transfer the question/answer improvisations to the recorder or pitched percussion instruments.

- Have students echo what you play in short melodic patterns using two or three pitches. When students are secure, ask them to improvise answers to questions you play.

STANDARD 3B

Improvising melodies, variations, and accompaniments: Students improvise simple rhythmic and melodic ostinato accompaniments.

Objective

- Students will create melodic, rhythmic, and movement ostinatos to accompany the song "Every Mornin'."

Materials

- Unpitched percussion instruments

- "Every Mornin'," in *Share the Music,* Grade 6 (New York: Macmillan/McGraw-Hill, 1995); or *World of Music,* Grade 2 and Grade 5 (Parsippany, NJ: Silver Burdett Ginn, 1991)

Prior Knowledge and Experiences

- Students have learned "Every Mornin'" in a previous class.

- Students have played rhythm instruments (both specific instrument parts and free exploration/creative playing) and can verbalize reasons for their musical preferences.

- Students have sung and played melodic ostinatos to accompany various songs.

Procedures

1. Invite students to review "Every Mornin'" by singing the song together. Then ask students to sing the words "Every Mornin'" on the tonic/resting tone (creating an ostinato on middle C using the rhythm of the first measure) while you sing the familiar melody.

2. Identify the part the students have sung as a melodic ostinato. Ask students to list examples of other melodic ostinatos they have played or sung. After the students have listed several, ask them to determine a definition of melodic ostinato with a partner and then to share their definitions with the class. Divide the class into two groups. Have one group sing the melodic ostinato, performed earlier, while the other sings "Every Mornin'"; then have the students switch parts.

3. Ask students to discuss a possible definition of rhythmic ostinato with their partners and then invite them to share their definitions with the class. Have them create rhythm ostinatos (employing body percussion) to accompany the song. (Point out that the melodic ostinato was part of the song and that a rhythm ostinato may also be a rhythm pattern from the song.) Ask several students to share their ostinatos with the class. Choose one ostinato and ask students to select an instrument appropriate for it. Sing the song with everyone performing the rhythm ostinato (some on instruments and some on body percussion).

4. Repeat this process for a movement ostinato. Ask students to discuss a definition, to create a movement ostinato on their own, and then to select one to accompany the song. After students have performed the song with movement ostinato, ask them to tell their partners the similarities and differences among the three kinds of ostinatos that have been demonstrated.

5. Divide the class into groups of six. Ask each group to improvise three ostinatos—one melodic, one rhythmic, and one movement—to perform with the song "Every Mornin'." All three ostinatos must be performed together by the group while the class sings the song. Give groups a specific amount of time (for example, ten minutes) in which to work.

6. At the end of the specified work time, have each group perform its ostinato while the class sings the song. At the end of each performance, ask class members to assess whether the group has met the criteria of improvising the three different ostinatos. Have each group assess how well the ostinato patterns it created fit with the song.

Indicators of Success

- Students verbally define or describe melodic, rhythmic, and movement ostinatos.

- Students improvise the three different types of ostinatos specified in the lesson.

- Improvised ostinatos are suitable for accompanying "Every Mornin'."

Follow-up

- Have students improvise ostinatos for other familiar songs. Ask students to notate ostinato patterns they have created and then to select several to rehearse with the song for a public performance.

STANDARD 3C

Improvising melodies, variations, and accompaniments: Students improvise simple rhythmic variations and simple melodic embellishments on familiar melodies.

Objective

- Students will improvise melodic and rhythmic embellishments for the song "This Train."

Materials

- "This Train," in *Share the Music*, Grade 5 (New York: Macmillan/McGraw-Hill, 1995); *Music and You*, Grade 6 (New York: Macmillan/McGraw-Hill, 1991); or *World of Music*, Grade 5 (Parsippany, NJ: Silver Burdett Ginn, 1991)

Prior Knowledge and Experiences

- Students have learned the song "This Train" during a previous class.

Procedures

1. Invite students to review "This Train" by singing the song together. Using student texts, have them follow the notation as they sing.

2. Tell the students that you will be singing the song with two changes in it. Ask them to listen and snap their fingers twice when they hear the changes you have made. Perform the song with two rhythmic alterations (for example, begin with a rest instead of singing the first note on the beat, or add dotted rhythms). Have the students identify where the alterations occurred.

3. Ask the students to listen again and decide, with a partner, whether the melody or the rhythm has been changed. Perform the rhythmically altered version of the song again and allow students time to discuss their answers with their partners. After listening to the students' answers, show them the rhythmic alternations by singing the original phrase and then the altered phrase.

4. Repeat the process to demonstrate melodic alterations of the song. Ask students to find alternations in your model; then have them determine whether the alterations are rhythmic or melodic. Demonstrate original and altered phrases to illustrate melodic embellishment.

5. Divide students into cooperative groups of three. Invite each trio to create its own improvised embellishments or alterations of "This Train." (Do not use student texts; rather, encourage the students to create their embellishments or alterations by ear.) Give the students a time limit for their work (for example, five to seven minutes).

6. At the end of the specified time, invite trios to sing their improvised versions of "This Train" for the class. Encourage class members to critically analyze each performance, determining whether the melody or rhythm (or both) was altered by the group and whether each trio's embellishments were in the style of the song.

Indicators of Success

- Students improvise rhythmic and melodic embellishments for "This Train."

- Students correctly identify rhythmic and melodic embellishments in a familiar song when they hear them.

Follow-up

- Allow students to improvise embellishments for other familiar songs. If students can play a melody on a recorder or xylophone, encourage them to try an instrumental improvisation.

- Provide students with listening examples of singers and instrumentalists embellishing or improvising on familiar melodies.

STANDARD 3D

Improvising melodies, variations, and accompaniments: Students improvise short songs and instrumental pieces using a variety of sound sources, including traditional sounds, nontraditional sounds available in the classroom, body sounds, and sounds produced by electronic means.

Objectives

- Students will improvise, with a partner, an accompaniment pattern using nontraditional sounds.
- Each student will improvise an eight-beat solo using the voice or an instrument.
- Students will create a short piece using their improvisations.

Materials

- Classroom instruments
- Non-instrument sound sources in the room
- Videocassette recorder and monitor
- Camcorder and blank tape
- Simple thirty-two-beat teacher- or student-composed rhythm piece that can be used as an accompaniment

Prior Knowledge and Experiences

- Students have improvised eight-beat rhythms in question/answer style.
- Students understand the terms "solo" and "accompaniment."
- Students have experience performing with various classroom instruments.
- Students can perform a simple thirty-two-beat teacher- or student-composed rhythm piece that will be used as an accompaniment in this lesson.

Procedures

1. Invite students to find sounds or sound sources in the classroom that are not instrument or voice sounds and to select one they like best. After the students have had an opportunity to explore, ask them to improvise an eight-beat rhythm using the sound they have found.

2. Have students share their eight-beat improvisations with a partner. Ask students to create a second eight-beat improvisation, this time taking turns with their partners. Invite pairs of students to share their improvisations with the class.

3. Help students review the thirty-two-beat rhythm composition they have learned in a previous class. Tell students that this composition will become an accompaniment for the improvised solos. Practice the thirty-two-beat composition so students can repeat it several times.

4. Tell students that one pair of students will take turns improvising eight-beat solos (called "trading" in jazz) while the class plays the accompaniment. The soloists may use traditional instruments or voices, as well as nontraditional sound sources. Practice with one pair improvising while the class plays the accompaniment.

5. Allow students to review their improvisations. Then appoint several pairs to be ready to improvise, one after the other, as the class plays the accompaniment. After pairs have taken a turn improvising, have them return to the accompaniment, or have students exchange improvising and accompanying roles after three or four pairs have played their improvised solos.

6. When students are comfortable, videotape their improvised solos with the accompaniment. After taping, allow them to watch the tape and evaluate their performances. Add the videotape to the class archives.

Indicators of Success

- Students can improvise for eight beats using both traditional and nontraditional sound sources.
- With practice, students can trade eight-beat improvised solos over an improvised accompaniment.
- Students can identify and describe whether their improvisations have met specified criteria (eight beats, nontraditional or traditional sound source).

Follow-up

- Encourage students to improvise solos using rhythm instruments or sounds they have found in the classroom to a given harmonic pattern, such as I-vi-IV-V^7 or the twelve-bar blues.

- Develop improvisations by adding melody instruments during a subsequent lesson.

STANDARD 4A

Composing and arranging music within specified guidelines: Students create and arrange music to accompany readings or dramatizations.

Objective

■ Students will create an accompaniment for a reading of *Listen to the Rain* using classroom instruments and voice sounds.

Materials

■ "Rain Song," in *The Music Connection,* Grade 4 (Parsippany, NJ: Silver Burdett Ginn, 1995)

■ *Listen to the Rain* by Bill Martin (New York: Henry Holt, 1988)

■ Classroom instruments, including a rainstick if available

Prior Knowledge and Experiences

■ Students can improvise with instruments freely and in a structured question/answer format.

■ Students have sung "Rain Song" during a previous class.

Procedures

1. Review "Rain Song" at the beginning of class. After the students have sung the song, invite them to list on the chalkboard or on a chart all the words they can think of to describe different kinds of rain (for example, "drizzle," "mist," "downpour," and "sprinkle").

2. Ask students to choose an instrument, voice, or nontraditional sound they can use to improvise a rain sound. After students have chosen their sounds, point to the words on the chalkboard or chart and have the students improvise sounds for that particular kind of rain. Ask students to use musical terms to describe how their improvisations for "drizzle," for example, are different from their improvisations for "downpour."

3. Read the book *Listen to the Rain.* Ask students to think about how to match their sounds to the text of the book while they listen.

4. Draw a time line on the board. Ask students to identify a key rain word on each page and write the key words in sequence on the time line. Have the students, while working in small groups, copy the time line onto a chart and then add musical symbols and terms to it (for example, dynamic symbols, tempo terms, instruments, notation, and icons) to compose an accompaniment while you read the book. Allow groups some time to practice their compositions.

5. Ask groups to share their compositions with the class while you or a class member reads the book. Place each group's composition chart so that the entire class can see it as they perform. After each performance, invite class members to analyze the group's chart and its performance, discussing the parts they liked and why they liked them, and giving friendly suggestions for improvement.

Indicators of Success

■ Students can compose and perform music to accompany a reading of *Listen to the Rain.*

■ Students' composition charts effectively show their musical ideas for accompanying a reading of *Listen to the Rain.* Students use musical terms, such as dynamic and tempo terms, to critique their own compositions and the compositions of other groups.

Follow-up

- Have the class choose ideas from various group compositions to combine into a class composition.

- Use the symbols, icons, and notation from the group compositions to write the class composition on the time line (which has been written on the board earlier in the lesson).

- Videotape group or class compositions and store them in the class archives.

- On another day, invite small groups to create accompaniments to other books, using a different book for each group.

STANDARD 4B

Composing and arranging music within specified guidelines: Students create and arrange short songs and instrumental pieces within specified guidelines.

Objectives

- Students will demonstrate understanding of a composer's use of tempo to generate a particular effect by listening to and analyzing a song with tempo changes.
- Students will compose an original work that includes a tempo change.

Materials

- Recording of Johannes Brahms's "Hungarian Dance no. 6"
- Recording of "Boa Constrictor," from *Peter, Paul, and Mommy* by Peter, Paul, and Mary (Warner Brothers 1785)
- Audio-playback equipment
- Assorted classroom instruments, both pitched and unpitched
- Chalkboard or chart (see Step 2)

Prior Knowledge and Experiences

- Students have experience finding and moving to the beat.
- Students recognize tempo changes in music and are familiar with the idea that a single piece of music can change tempo several times.

Procedures

1. Ask students to pat the beat on their laps as they listen to the opening minute of Brahms's "Hungarian Dance no. 6." After the students have listened to the piece, ask them to describe the tempo of the music. (The tempo changes from slow to fast and back again several times.) While standing or sitting in a circle, have the students pass a ball to the beat of the music. At the conclusion of the piece, ask students to describe what happened to their levels of excitement and concentration as the tempo of the music changed.

2. Draw three different series of marks indicating beats on the chalkboard or on a chart:

   Choice A: | | | | | |||||||||

   Choice B: | | | | STOP ||||||||

   Choice C: | | | | | | | |||||||||| ||||||

   Tell students that they are going to hear a song they may already know in which the tempo changes from slow to fast. Ask the students to listen to the song and keep the beat by patting. They must decide, by the end of the song, which set of beat patterns written on the board best shows how the music changes tempo—all of a sudden (A), after a pause (B), or gradually increasing in speed (C). They must also decide why the composer decided to change tempo during the song.

3. Play the recording of "Boa Constrictor." After the students have listened to the song, ask them to tell a partner which choice of beat patterns best matches the song and why. (C is the correct answer.) After the students have discussed their answers with a partner, have them share their ideas with the class. Then ask the students to share their ideas regarding why the composer decided to change tempo in this song.

4. On the same day or during the next class, ask students to work in groups of four to six to compose their own music that creates a similar effect—a change of tempo from slow to fast. Students may use both acoustic and electronic instruments—whatever is available in the classroom—as well as voice sounds. Write the assign-

ment on the board as follows:

1. Find your group members.

2. Choose instruments and a work area in the room.

3. Compose a slow section for your composition.

4. Decide whether the fast section will have the same music or different music than the slow section.

5. Play the slow section. Play the fast section.

6. Decide which beat pattern you will use to move from the slow section to the fast section: A (abrupt or instant change), B (change after a pause), or C (gradually speeding up).

7. Rehearse your composition so you can perform it for the class.

8. Please be ready in ten minutes. *(Note: More time will result in more complex compositions.)*

5. At the end of the specified work time, invite students to share their compositions with the class. After each group performs, discuss the decisions made by the group. Did they complete the assignment correctly? How did they choose to work on their compositions? Which plan for changing tempo did they choose? How did they know when to change tempo? What else did they change from their A to B sections in addition to tempo? After all the compositions have been performed, ask additional questions, such as: How was one group's piece different from another's? What effect do the tempo changes have?

Indicators of Success

- Students can respond to tempo changes in music by moving and can describe tempo changes verbally.

- Student compositions include tempo changes. Students can identify the characteristics of tempo changes (abrupt, after a pause, or gradual) in their own and others' compositions and can describe the perceived effect of tempo changes.

Follow-up

- Have students devise a means of notating their compositions; then ask them to exchange their scores and perform a composition written by another group.

- Have students compose similar short pieces with dynamic changes instead of tempo changes.

STANDARD 4C

*Composing and arranging music within specified guidelines: Students use
a variety of sound sources when composing.*

Objective

- Students will create, perform, and evaluate an original accompaniment to a haiku.

Materials

- Japanese folk song with which students are familiar

- Assorted unpitched percussion instruments, such as sticks, drums, woodblocks, castanets, sand blocks, and wooden and rubber mallets

- The following haiku by James W. Hackett (from *The Zen Haiku and Other Zen Poems of J. W. Hackett*), to be written on the chalkboard or on an overhead transparency or chart:

  Crow pecks into the sand,
  Swallows what he finds, then
  Shudders all over.

  Copyright © 1983 by James W. Hackett. Used by permission.

- Overhead projector (optional)

Prior Knowledge and Experiences

- Students have had experiences with choral speaking, cooperative learning, and playing classroom instruments.

- Students have learned one or more Japanese folk songs in the previous class period.

Procedures

1. Have students review the Japanese folk song they learned during the previous class period by singing it together. Ask students to look at the song lyrics in their student texts or on a chart or overhead transparency. Have them identify words that refer to nature and then determine how the emphasis on nature may influence performance. Then have them sing the song again.

2. Direct students' attention to the haiku that has been written on the chalkboard, chart, or overhead transparency. Have them read the poem silently. Provide a brief background on the origin of the haiku. (Haiku is a Japanese form of poetry with seventeen syllables in a three-line form and is usually—but not always—a 5–7–5 arrangement of syllables; it is also nature based.) Ask the students to determine the number of syllables in this particular haiku (seventeen) and the arrangement of syllables in the line (6–6–5). In addition, have them look for words referring to nature.

3. Read the poem expressively to the class. Have the students explain which words suggest sounds to them (pecks, swallows, shudders). Have the class practice reading the poem aloud, slowly, and with expression. Tell students that they are going to create an accompaniment for the poem.

4. Show students an assortment of unpitched percussion instruments and elicit suggestions for which instrument (or combination of instruments) could suggest each of the sounds. Tell students that they may also use other materials in the classroom for inventing sounds (for example, "pecks" might be sticks tapping on a soft notebook cover). Have several students try out their ideas using different instruments, making each sound last for several seconds. Ask students to evaluate the appropriateness of each sound.

5. Select three players for each word. Have these students play as the class reads the poem aloud. Guide students in making their playing continuous (not just a single stroke or tap). Help them overlap their sounds, producing yet another timbre. Have the students evaluate their performance for dynamics, balance, length of sound, and suitable entrance/exit. Repeat as needed. Consider adding an introduction and a coda.

6. Divide the class into groups of five students. Give them one or two minutes to designate group members as follows: one poem reader, three instrumentalists, one secretary. Tell students that each group will create its own composition using the same haiku. The secretary will write down the reasons for their choices of instruments and combinations of sounds.

7. Have groups follow the whole-class procedure used previously: select/try instruments, add poems, evaluate. Be sure they realize that each group will later perform its sound piece for the whole class and explain its choices. Establish a time frame for working on each task as needed.

8. After a final run through, have students perform for each other, hearing each group's justifications and noticing the special timbre of each instrument and combination.

Indicators of Success

- Students successfully create and perform small-group compositions using haikus and sound sources of their choice expressively.

- Students justify their choices of instruments and sounds using appropriate music terminology.

Follow-up

- Have students read different haikus and select one to create their own compositions.

- Have students write haikus in the classroom and bring them to music class for use in their own music compositions.

STANDARD 5A

Reading and notating music: Students read whole, half, dotted half, quarter, and eighth notes and rests in 2/4, 3/4, and 4/4 meter signatures.

Objective

- Students will clap four-beat rhythm patterns containing whole, half, dotted half, quarter, and eighth notes and rests in a given tempo.

Materials

- Familiar song that includes the rhythms students are learning

- Several four-beat flash cards for each set of two students (rhythms on the flash cards include rhythms present in the familiar song selected for the lesson)

- Recording of "Latin Rock," from *Music for Movement* by James Froseth and Phyllis S. Weikart (GIA Publications MLR 187), or a similar commercial or teacher-generated sound track specifically designed for students to play or clap along with

- Audio-playback equipment

Procedures

1. Lead the students in echo clapping as a warm-up activity. Have them practice a rhythm round. Then have students work in pairs to practice the four-beat rhythm flash cards.

2. Ask students to define rhythm and beat, and then have them describe the difference between the two using words, movement, or performance. Play the recording you have selected or the sound track you have generated and ask the students to tap the steady beat.

3. Tell the students that they are going to read and clap the rhythm patterns they have practiced as they are accompanied by music that has a steady beat. Tell them that they will clap one pattern and then wait four beats, or rest, before clapping the next pattern.

4. Start the recording. Hold the rhythm flash cards and ask the students to clap the rhythm written on the first card, rest for four beats, and then clap the rhythm written on the second card. Continue with the cards and the pattern of rhythms and rests.

5. When the students are comfortable and confident performing the rhythms together, ask them to repeat the activity while working in pairs. One student holds the flash cards and moves them ahead during the rests while the other student claps the patterns. Then have the students switch roles.

6. Look at the notation for a familiar song that includes the rhythms the students have just practiced. Have them clap and say the rhythm of the song. Then sing the song together, first tapping the beat, then the rhythm. Challenge students to tap the beat with their feet and the rhythm with their hands as they sing.

Indicators of Success

- Students accurately identify and perform the rhythm on the flash cards with a steady beat and at the tempo of the recorded accompaniment track.

- Students accurately read and perform the rhythms in a familiar song.

Prior Knowledge and Experiences

- Students have performed echo clapping games, can distinguish between "beat" and "rhythm" and have had experience reading four-beat patterns containing whole, half, dotted half, quarter, and eighth notes and rests in 2/4, 3/4, and 4/4 meter signatures.

- Students can identify note names and note values using both standard notation and stem notation.

Follow-up

- Eliminate the four beats of rest between the flash card patterns and move directly from one pattern to the next. Hint: The person holding the cards will need to shift to the next card on the third beat of each pattern.

- Show students the rhythm of a song they have not yet learned, but which is composed entirely of rhythms with which they are familiar. Have them read and tap or clap the rhythm, and then teach them the melody by rote.

- Have students look and listen for familiar rhythms in various listening examples. Compositions with repeated rhythms are particularly useful, such as Ludwig van Beethoven's Second Movement (A section) of Symphony no. 7; Edvard Grieg's "In the Hall of the Mountain King," from *Peer Gynt Suite no. 1*; Franz Joseph Haydn's Second Movement (theme only) of Symphony no. 94 in G Major ("Surprise"); Dmitri Kabalevsky's "March," from *The Comedians*; and Piotr Illyich Tchaikovsky's "Dance of the Sugar Plum Fairy," from *The Nutcracker Suite*.

STANDARD 5B

*Reading and notating music: Students use a system (syllables, numbers, or letters)
to read simple pitch notation in the treble clef in major keys.*

Objective

- Students aurally identify, notate, and read a *do-la_1-sol_1* (1-6_1-5_1) melodic pattern.

Materials

- Several familiar songs that use the descending melodic pattern *do-la_1-sol_1* (1-6_1-5_1), including the song "Hill an' Gully," in *The Music Connection*, Grade 3 (Parsippany, NJ: Silver Burdett Ginn, 1995); *Share the Music*, "Songs to Sing and Read" (New York: Macmillan/McGraw-Hill, 1995); *Music and You*, Grade 4 (New York: Macmillan/McGraw-Hill, 1991); or *World of Music*, Grade 3 (Parsippany, NJ: Silver Burdett Ginn, 1991)
- Felt staff and note manipulatives or laminated staff paper with note manipulatives

Prior Knowledge and Experiences

- Students use a number or syllable system for learning melodic patterns.
- Students have sung the *do-la_1-sol_1* (1-6_1-5_1 or do, low la, low sol) melodic pattern in several songs, but have not yet notated it.
- Students know the song "Hill an' Gully."

Procedures

1. Ask the students to echo a series of melodic patterns in which *do-la_1-sol_1* (1-6_1-5_1) is included as a warm-up exercise. Use the system (numbers or syllables) with which the students are familiar.

2. Show the students an iconic representation of the pattern (for example, three circles on a descending diagonal, with greater space between the first two circles). Have the students sing *do-la_1-sol_1* (1-6_1-5_1) while looking at the icon.

3. Ask the students to sing "Hill an' Gully." Then have them identify the *do-la_1-sol_1* (1-6_1-5_1) pattern aurally each time it occurs in the song. (*Note: It occurs three times, with some of the notes repeated the second and third times.*)

4. Help students discover how the *do-la_1-sol_1* (1-6_1-5_1) pattern translates to notes on a staff. Then ask each student to notate the melodic pattern with felt staff manipulatives or laminated staff paper and erasable markers or manipulatives.

5. Sing "Hill an' Gully" again (using the words), and have students point to the *do-la_1-sol_1* (1-6_1-5_1) pattern on their felt or laminated staves each time as it occurs.

6. Ask students to look at a notated copy of the song and find the *do-la_1-sol_1* (1-6_1-5_1) pattern. Sing the song and substitute the solfège or numbers for the pattern when it occurs.

7. Ask students to find the same pattern aurally and in the printed music of other familiar songs.

Indicators of Success

- Students aurally identify, notate, and read the *do-la_1-sol_1* melodic pattern in familiar songs.

Follow-up

■ Present a new song in which the *do-la₁-sol₁* (1-6_1-5_1) pattern or some rhythmic variant of the pattern occurs. Ask the students to find the pattern and use it to help them learn the new song or phrases of the new song. Examples of appropriate songs include "Turn the Glasses Over," in *Just Five,* compiled by Robert E. Kersey (Miami, FL: Belwin-Mills, 1972); "Alabama Girl," in *Folk Songs North America Sings* by Richard Johnston (Toronto: Caveat Music Publishers, 1984); "Amasee," in *Sail Away: 155 American Folk Songs to Sing, Read, and Play,* edited by Eleanor G. Locke (New York: Boosey & Hawkes, 1989); "King Kong Kitchie," in *150 American Folk Songs to Sing, Read, and Play,* edited by Peter Erdei and Katalin Komlos (New York: Boosey & Hawkes, 1974).

STANDARD 5C

Reading and notating music: Students identify symbols and traditional terms referring to dynamics, tempo, and articulation and interpret them correctly when performing.

Objective

- Students will recognize Italian terms and metronome markings as tempo designations in music and will determine appropriate tempos for familiar songs.

Materials

- The "Crawdad" song, in *The Music Connection,* Grade 4 (Parsippany, NJ: Silver Burdett Ginn, 1995); *Share the Music,* "Songs to Sing and Read" (New York: Macmillan/McGraw-Hill, 1995); *Music and You,* Grade 3 (New York: Macmillan/McGraw-Hill, 1991); or *World of Music,* Grade 4 (Parsippany, NJ: Silver Burdett Ginn, 1991)

- List of songs familiar to students

- At least one metronome, more if possible

- Example of music with tempo markings

- Chalkboard

Prior Knowledge and Experiences

- Students have a working knowledge of the concept of fast and slow and the term "tempo."

- Students can sing the "Crawdad" song.

Procedures

1. Invite the students to sing the "Crawdad" song as a warm-up activity for the lesson.

2. Show the students the metronome; tell them what it is, what it is called, and demonstrate how it works. Point out the numbers and the Italian words that designate various tempos.

3. Ask the students to sing the "Crawdad" song and to tap the steady beat. After they have sung the song, invite one or more students (depending on the number of metronomes available) to match the metronome speed with the steady beat tapped by the class during the song.

4. When the metronomes are set, ask the students to look on the metronome for the Italian word that indicates that tempo. Write the Italian term and the number of beats per minute on the board. (Numbers may not agree exactly if you are using more than one metronome. Choose one of the numbers given by the students when this occurs.)

5. Invite students to try singing the "Crawdad" song at other tempos. Ask a student to look closely at the metronome and select a faster or slower tempo. Write that Italian term and the corresponding number on the board. Start the metronome and ask students to listen to the beat. Then stop the metronome and have the students sing the "Crawdad" song at that tempo while patting the beat on their laps. After the students have tried two or three different tempos, ask them to tell a partner which tempo they liked best and why.

6. Choose a song from a list of those familiar to the students. Repeat the same procedure to find a tempo for the song. Continue the process of experimenting with other songs and tempos, writing the corresponding terms and numerical indications on the board. Then teach the class a new song. Invite the students to determine an appropriate tempo, asking them to give supporting reasons for the tempo they choose. Identify this tempo with the correct Italian term.

7. Help students find examples of tempo markings in their student texts. Show them another piece of music, possibly orchestral or choral, that has a metronome marking and tempo designations using Italian terms.

Indicators of Success

- Students recognize different tempos in familiar songs and use appropriate terminology to describe the tempos.
- Students transfer their learning when selecting expressive tempos for new and familiar songs.

Follow-up

- Create opportunities for each student to experiment with the metronome.
- Provide MIDI experiences for manipulating the tempo of songs.

STANDARD 5D

Reading and notating music: Students use standard symbols to notate meter, rhythm, pitch, and dynamics in simple patterns presented by the teacher.

Objective

- Students will identify random pitches from the major scale.

Materials

- Apple IIe or Macintosh computers
- *DoReMi* computer program by Bruce Benward and David B. Williams (Bellevue, WA: Temporal Acuity Products, 1992) (Note: Substitute other computers and age-appropriate notation programs depending on the technology available.)
- Felt staff manipulatives or laminated staff paper with note manipulatives or erasable markers
- DAC board (optional)
- Sound amplification system (optional)
- Large monitor or PC viewer (optional)
- Student journals

Prior Knowledge and Experiences

- Students are familiar with solfège syllables and know the Curwen hand signs.

Procedures

1. Demonstrate the computer-assisted *DoReMi* notation game for the students. (The computer plays a scale and then plays a single note. The player must identify by solfège syllable the pitch played by the computer.)

2. Divide the class into teams of four students. Guide students in determining who will fill these roles:

   Listener—this person names the solfège syllable of the pitch played by the computer

   Keyboarder—this person enters the answer on the keyboard

   Signer—this person indicates the Curwen hand sign for the pitch

   Scribe—this person notates the pitch on the staff

   Encourage the students to ask for help from their teammates when they need it. Also encourage students not to give help until it is requested. Trade roles at agreed upon intervals so that each student has aural and kinesthetic interaction with the pitches.

3. Have students play the *DoReMi* game. Ask the teams to record their progress in their journals. When the students complete one level, have them move to a more difficult level. Teams may stay intact or be reconfigured, depending on social goals for cooperative learning.

4. To help students apply what they have learned, have them review a familiar song, looking at the notation in their music books. Ask students to identify the notes in a particular phrase using solfège syllables and Curwen hand signals, and then sing the phrase using solfège.

Indicators of Success

- Students recognize, name, sign, and notate pitches in the *DoReMi* game and within the context of a song.

Follow-up

- Extend music learning beyond the music class period by making the *DoReMi* program available for individual reinforcement in the school's computer lab, the music room, or another classroom.

STANDARD 6A

Listening to, analyzing, and describing music: Students identify simple music forms when presented aurally.

Objective

- Students will identify characteristics that enable them to make decisions about the form of the composition in listening examples longer than classroom songs.

Materials

- Resonator bells, xylophones, and recorders
- Recording of "Circus Music," from *The Red Pony Suite* by Aaron Copland
- Chalkboard
- Student journals

Prior Knowledge and Experiences

- Students have moved to, analyzed, and identified songs with ABA form.

Procedures

1. After a discussion of the use of fanfares, invite students to produce a one-pitch fanfare ("Tah dah!") using instruments such as resonator bells, xylophones, and recorders.

2. Have students listen to "Circus Music" and count the number of fanfares they hear. Ask them to hold up the appropriate number of fingers to tell how many fanfares they have heard. If students do not agree, have them listen again. If necessary, assist them with counting the fanfares as they occur.

3. Draw a horizontal line across the chalkboard. Invite students to listen to "Circus Music" again, this time indicating where to place the fanfare marks (FF) to interrupt the horizontal line. The marks show when the fanfares occur during the music.

4. Play the theme from the first section (A), and ask the students to select an icon to represent this theme. (It could be the letter "A" or a shape or symbol of the students' choice.)

5. Ask the students to identify the first theme as they listen to the piece again. As they identify it, place the icon they have selected on the line on the chalkboard to show at which point the theme occurs. Invite the students to create a movement to perform during the two sections that contain this first theme.

6. Ask the students to listen to "Circus Music" again, performing their movement during the appropriate sections and stopping at the contrasting (middle) section.

7. Invite the students to select an icon for the contrasting section. Write it at the appropriate place on the line. Ask the students to label the sections of the piece with letters, if they have not already done so (ABA).

8. Encourage the students to imagine that they are the composer of the piece and to give the composition a name. Then tell them Copland's title for the piece, describing the context for which he wrote it. Listen again to close the lesson.

Indicators of Success

- Students create appropriate icons and movements for the listening example and accurately identify the three sections (ABA) of this piece.

Follow-up

- Transfer this process to identifying sections of other ABA compositions. Have students draw lines, icons, and letters designating the sections of the pieces in their personal journals. Examples of ABA compositions include: Edvard Grieg's "Norwegian Dance no. 2"; Dmitri Kabalevsky's "Gallop," from *The Comedians;* Modest Mussorgsky's "Ballet of the Unhatched Chicks," from *Pictures at an Exhibition;* Carl Orff's "Tanz," from *Carmina Burana;* Sergei Prokofiev's "Departure," from *Winter Bonfire Suite;* and Igor Stravinsky's "Berceuse," from *Firebird Suite.*

STANDARD 6B

Listening to, analyzing, and describing music: Students demonstrate perceptual skills by moving, by answering questions about, and by describing aural examples of music of various styles representing diverse cultures.

Objective

- Students will improvise movement, show the rhythm of the melody, create an icon chart, and describe the qualities of a piece that combines a string quartet and African drums.

Materials

- Recording of "Mai Nozipo" by Dumisani Maraire, from *Pieces of Africa*, performed by the Kronos Quartet, Elektra/Nonesuch 979275-2
- Audio-playback equipment

Prior Knowledge and Experiences

- Students have experience improvising rhythms and creating icon charts.

Procedures

1. As the students enter the room, play the recording of "Mai Nozipo." Invite the students to improvise movement to the music.

2. Ask the students to listen again to the first section and find the repeated rhythm of the A section of the melody. Have them tap, pat, or move the rhythm as they identify it.

3. After the students have listened a second time, ask them to create an iconic or graphic chart that shows the repeated rhythm to which they have listened and moved. Allow students to listen to the A section of the music again as they create their charts. When they have finished, have them practice pointing to their charts as they listen.

4. Ask students to exchange their charts. Then have them listen to the music again, this time following someone else's chart.

5. Ask the students to describe the rhythm of the melody (sycopated) and other qualities of the music, such as the instrumentation (various African percussion instruments and traditional string quartet), form (ABA, with a melody repeated many times in the A sections), tempo (fast-slow-fast), and dynamics (loud-soft-loud).

Indicators of Success

- Students identify and respond to a repeated rhythm by moving appropriately, creating an icon chart, and responding to an icon chart drawn by another student.
- Students describe various characteristics of the music using musical terms learned in class as well as in their own words.

Follow-up

- Create a similar learning experience using a music example from a different culture (for example, a recording of the traditional Chinese tune "Purple Bamboo Melody") or a composition that fuses two cultures (for example, "Kurski Funk," from *Earth Beat,* by Winter, Halley, and Castro-Neves, performed by the Paul Winter Consort, Living Music Records LD0015). Have students listen for characteristics of the melody, rhythm, form, or other musical qualities.

STANDARD 6C

Listening to, analyzing, and describing music: Students use appropriate terminology in explaining music, music notation, musical instruments and voices, and music performances.

Objective

- Students will work in cooperative groups to listen to and describe a music performance.

Materials

- Recording of Dmitri Kabalevsky's "Gallop," from *The Comedians*
- Audio-playback equipment
- Chalkboard
- Student journals

Prior Knowledge and Experiences

- Students have discussed the basic elements of rhythm, tempo, dynamics, melody, and instrumental tone color.

Procedures

1. List these topics on the board—tempo, dynamics, instruments, melody, and rhythm. After students have formed home-base groups of five, have each student choose one of the five topics.

2. Tell students that they will hear a new piece of music. Each person is to become an "expert" on his or her topic. Each student will teach the other members of the group what he or she has learned about the topic from listening to the selection.

3. Play the recording. Give the students time to make notes on their topics on a card or in their music journals. Have the student experts share what they learned about "Gallop" so far with the other members of their home-base group.

4. Invite students to leave their home-base groups and get into groups with other experts who share information about their topics—for example, all the melody experts meet together. (The process of moving from home-base groups to expert groups and back again is a cooperative learning technique called "jigsawing.")

5. Provide each group of experts with a list of questions about its topic to prod thinking. (For example, questions for the dynamics group may include "What dynamic level does this piece begin with?" and "Do the dynamics change during this composition? How?") Play the selection again for expert groups to review.

6. Ask students to discuss their topics again in their expert group. Then have all students return to their home-base groups and share new and reinforced information from all five expert groups.

7. As they work in home-base groups, have students listen once more to the music and write questions about the music that can be answered based on the day's listening and discussion. Circulate the questions to other home-base groups or use questions for whole-class review and closure. Resolve any additional questions that arise by listening again.

Indicators of Success

- Students identify and explain to each other the characteristics of the music using appropriate terms.
- Students answer the questions posed by the other students about the music.

Follow-up

- Tell the students the origin of the music, the definition of a suite, and information about Kabalevsky. Then listen to the recording again.

- Play the first eight melody notes of the A section of the "Gallop" on mallet percussion instruments before the students have listened to the music; then play the notes with the music.

- Play the "March" from the same suite and repeat the cooperative learning jigsaw process.

STANDARD 6D

Listening to, analyzing, and describing music: Students identify the sounds of a variety of instruments, including many orchestra and band instruments, and instruments from various cultures, as well as children's voices and male and female adult voices.

Objective

- After listening to aural examples, students will identify a variety of Native American musical instruments.

Materials

- Recording of "Makoce Wakan," from *Red Thunder* (Canyon Records ETR 7916, available from Canyon Records and Indian Arts, 4143 North 16th Street, Phoenix, AZ 85016; telephone 602-266-4823)
- Audio-playback equipment
- Native American instruments or pictures of them from *Moving within the Circle* by Bryan Burton (Danbury, CT: World Music Press, 1993)

Prior Knowledge and Experiences

- Students have listened to and played a number of Native American instruments, including drums, rattles, and flutes.

Procedures

1. Lead students in a brief review of the instruments commonly used in Native American music. Show examples of these instruments when available or use illustrations—enlarge the pictures when possible for easy viewing.

2. Play "Makoce Wakan." Ask students to listen for different types of instruments and list them in their journals.

3. As students work in small groups, ask them to share what they have heard with group members by identifying by name an instrument they have heard, describing the sound of that instrument, and pointing to the correct photo of that instrument. (Instruments in this piece are: large drum, small hand drum, rawhide rattles, Native American flutes, and eagle bone whistles.)

4. Review the instruments in this piece with the class as a whole by playing the recording and having the students point to the pictures when a specific instrument is playing.

5. Listen to other examples of Native American music from *Red Thunder* or from the recording that accompanies *Moving within the Circle*. Have students continue to identify instruments played in these recordings using the same process.

Indicators of Success

- Students identify visually and aurally the Native American instruments played in "Makoce Wakan" and other recorded examples.

Follow-up

- Ask students to identify the number of sections in "Makoce Wakan." (There are three, with the third being a repeat of the first. Although this might be identified as ABA in Western terms, it would not be called that in Native American description.) Ask the students to describe the similarities and differences between the sections.

- With the aid of local community resources, help students collect information about the history and lifeways of Native American people in your region.

STANDARD 6E

Listening to, analyzing, and describing music: Students respond through purposeful movement to selected prominent music characteristics or to specific music events while listening to music.

Objective

■ Students will aurally recognize phrases in music and respond with expressive movement.

Materials

■ Recording of Prelude in A by Frédéric Chopin

■ Audio-playback equipment

Prior Knowledge and Experiences

■ The students have sung, moved to, and identified phrases in songs and are comfortable with expressive movement.

Procedures

1. Review the concept of phrase by singing a familiar song with clear phrase structure. Ask students to work with a partner to determine the beginning and ending of each phrase. Have the pairs share their answers with the class. Ask the students to sing the song again and move their arms in simple arches to indicate the phrases.

2. While listening to a recording of Chopin's Prelude in A, have the students use the same arched arm movements to indicate the beginning and ending of each phrase. Play the recording again and repeat the movement activity, asking the students to quietly count to themselves the number of phrases in the music (eight).

3. Play the recording again. This time, have students use more elaborate hand and arm movements for each phrase to indicate other features of the music, such as melody or expressive qualities. During another listening, invite them to move around the room to the phrases of the music, pausing at the end of each. Encourage students to pause at different levels (high, middle, and low), and then turn and move in a different direction at the beginning of each new phrase.

4. After listening and moving, ask students to describe the length of the phrases in this composition (they are all the same). Ask them to listen again and determine whether the melody and rhythm are the same in each phrase as well (the rhythm is the same, but the melody changes). Continue by asking for information about dynamics and tempo, if time permits.

5. Close the lesson by playing the recording again and having the students move, showing their new knowledge about the music. After they have listened and moved, have them describe what they have learned to a partner.

Indicators of Success

■ Students accurately describe and demonstrate musical phrases through expressive movement.

■ Students identify same phrase lengths, repeated rhythm, and changing melody as characteristics of this composition.

Follow-up

- Use the same procedure to move to the phrases of a familiar song or a different listening example. Songs may include "America, the Beautiful," in *The Music Connection,* Grades 3–8 (Parsippany, NJ: Silver Burdett Ginn, 1995), *Share the Music,* Grades 3–5 (New York: Macmillan/McGraw-Hill, 1995), *Music and You,* Grades 2, 4, 5, and 6 (New York: Macmillan/McGraw-Hill, 1991), or *World of Music,* Grades 3–8 (Parsippany, NJ: Silver Burdett Ginn, 1991); "Las estrellitas del cielo," in *The Music Connection,* Grade 4 (Parsippany, NJ: Silver Burdett Ginn, 1995); and "Sourwood Mountain," in *Share the Music,* Grade 4 (New York: Macmillan/McGraw-Hill, 1995) or *Music and You,* Grade 5 (New York: Macmillan/ McGraw-Hill, 1991). Listening examples may include Johann Sebastian Bach's "Jesu, Joy of Man's Desiring" (chorale); William Billings's "Chester" (chorale); Antonín Dvořák's "Largo," from Symphony no. 9 ("From the New World"); Duke Ellington's "Dooji-Wooji"; George Frideric Handel's "Minuet," from *Music for the Royal Fireworks;* Wolfgang Amadeus Mozart's "Minuet and Trio," from Symphony no. 39; and Camille Saint-Saëns's "The Swan," from *Carnival of the Animals.*

- Have students identify the number of phrases, similar or different lengths of phrases, and other prominent characteristics of the music.

STANDARD 7A

Evaluating music and music performances: Students devise criteria for evaluating performances and compositions.

Objective

- Students will develop and implement criteria for evaluating their vocal performance.

Materials

- Chalkboard or overhead projector and blank transparency
- Student journals

Prior Knowledge and Experiences

- Students know songs from memory that would be appropriate for a performance at a neighborhood mall or retirement community.
- Students are familiar with good singing and performance skills.

Procedures

1. Ask students to collaborate with you to select five songs from their repertoire that are appropriate for a short performance at a nearby mall or retirement community.

2. List the songs vertically down the left side of a blank matrix on the chalkboard or on an overhead transparency.

3. Have students work in small groups to develop the criteria or categories that will go across the top of the matrix to evaluate their performance of each song. Categories might include tone quality, diction, expression, and so on. Students develop a rating scale for the categories: for example, 1 = "needs improvement," 3 = "satisfactory," and 5 = "outstanding." For reference, have the students draw the matrix in their music journals and then write in the song titles and the evaluation criteria.

4. Practice the songs. Have each student evaluate each performance for the criteria across the top of the matrix. Each singer uses a "thumbs down" to signal #1, a "thumbs to the side" to signal #3, and a "thumbs up" to signal #5. Scan the class to see what most of the students have rated "diction," for example, and write that number in the matrix cell on the chalkboard or overhead transparency.

5. Give students a moment to reflect on their individual singing abilities after practicing one of the songs. Using the matrix they have copied into their journals, have each student evaluate his or her own singing.

6. At the end of the lesson, have the students look at the class matrix to become aware of which areas need improvement, and ask them to identify the songs that they believe need the most rehearsal during their next class meeting.

Indicators of Success

- Students develop a matrix that allows each member of the class to have input on the quality of the performance and that provides each student with clear information regarding areas that need improvement.

Follow-up

- With audio or video equipment, record the singing on the day the matrix was first created and at the time of performance. Ask the students to use the criteria they have listed across the top of the matrix to determine if they have demonstrated better singing and performance skills as a result of this self-evaluation process. Ask students what they would do to improve the process for the next performance.

- Develop a similar process for students to perform and evaluate their own compositions.

STANDARD 7B

Evaluating music and music performances: Students explain, using appropriate music terminology, their personal preferences for specific musical works and styles.

Objectives

- Students will listen to three recordings of the song "Getting to Know You" and will use appropriate music terminology to describe differences among the three and to tell which version they prefer.

Materials

- Three recordings of "Getting to Know You" (possibly one from a textbook series recording, one from a Broadway or movie sound track of *The King and I*, and the James Taylor version from *For Our Children,* Disney 60616-2)
- Audio-playback equipment
- Copies of Venn diagram

Prior Knowledge and Experiences

- Students are able to sing the song from memory.

Procedures

1. Tell the students that you have two recordings of the song "Getting to Know You." Their task will be to describe each recording, to tell how it is the same and different from the others, and to decide which recording they like better.

2. Divide the students into groups of three. Give each group a blank Venn diagram (see the example below). Tell students that they will listen to the first recording and write information about the music they hear in the left circle. Prior to their listening, give the students an opportunity to discuss with their groups what kinds of information they will listen for. For example, they might want to note what kind of voices are singing, which instruments are used in the accompaniment, and how many times the song is repeated.

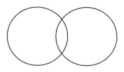

3. Play the first example for the class. Have the students write down what they have heard on the left side of the Venn diagram. Students may need to listen more than once. Encourage the students to work as teams and to share information. Individual students might listen for specific information and then share what they have heard within the group.

4. Tell the students that they will now hear a second recording of the same song. Ask them to write information about the second version on the right side of the Venn diagram. Play the second recording, and have the students record their information.

5. Ask the students to compare the two versions they have heard using the information they have collected on the Venn diagrams. Have them write the common features of the two versions in the intersection of the two circles. As they do this, have them cross off these common features on the left and right sides. The result should be unique features of the first version in the left circle, unique features of the second version in the right circle, and common features in the middle.

6. Ask the students to discuss the similarities and differences of the two versions in their groups and then to tell which one they prefer and why. Have the students share their findings with the class using appropriate music terminology.

7. On another day, play the recording of the third version of the song. Ask the students to compare the third version to the first two they have heard. Then have students select a favorite and justify their choice with musical vocabulary. They may do this orally or by writing in their music journals.

Indicators of Success

- Students successfully complete the collection and comparison of information and articulate their findings using age-appropriate music vocabulary.

Follow-up

- Repeat this activity using traditional and rock versions of a familiar song, two versions of an instrumental selection, or the same song performed in two or more cultural traditions.

STANDARD 8A

Understanding relationships between music, the other arts, and disciplines outside the arts: Students identify similarities and differences in the meanings of common terms used in the various arts.

Objective

- Students will describe and demonstrate the use of the word "color" in music and in art.

Materials

- Envelopes containing five pieces of paper in various hues of red, purple, and blue
- Recording of a familiar song that uses an adult voice independently and a children's chorus alone (for example, an adult singing the verse and children singing the refrain)
- Audio-playback equipment

Prior Knowledge and Experiences

- Students recognize and can label adult male and female and children's voices.
- Students understand the terms "verse" and "refrain."
- Students know specific color names, such as those found in a crayon box.

Procedures

1. As the students work in small groups, ask them to open the envelopes and examine the colored paper. Have them label each color as closely as possible (red, violet, magenta, burgundy, turquoise, blue-violet, and so on). Have them share their ideas; ask for words to describe the color differences. Don't expect consensus.

2. Tell the students that the shades of a color are sometimes similar but not identical—they may be identified as different hues of the color and are designated by individual color names (magenta, violet, and so on).

3. Invite students to listen to the recording and focus on the voices. Ask what kind of voice or voices are singing the verses and the refrain. Ask the students to describe how they have arrived at their answers. (They might say that the man's voice is lower or that the children's voices sound like theirs.)

4. Tell the students that singing voices are similar but not identical. The uniqueness of any singing voice may be identified as the "tone color" of that particular voice.

5. Reinforce the students' understanding with this activity: Place two children where they can't be seen (behind a standing bulletin board or at the back of the class). Ask each student to sing a simple phrase. Have the other children in the class determine which student sang first and which one sang second. At the end of the activity, ask students to develop their own definition of "tone color."

Indicators of Success

- Students describe and give examples of the use of the word "color" in the visual arts.
- Students describe and give examples of the use of the term "tone color" in music.

Follow-up

- On another day, have a similar discussion and use similar activities to investigate instrumental tone color (for example, have students listen to and identify the tone colors of brass family instruments; have students compare and contrast the plucked and bowed sounds of stringed instruments from various cultures).

STANDARD 8B

Understanding relationships between music, the other arts, and disciplines outside the arts: Students identify ways in which the principles and subject matter of other disciplines taught in the school are interrelated with those of music.

Objective

- Students will identify patterns in notation and number sequences as ways to solve musical and mathematical problems.

Materials

- "Billy Boy," in *The Music Connection,* Grade 3 (Parsippany, NJ: Silver Burdett Ginn, 1995); or *World of Music,* Grade 3 (Parsippany, NJ: Silver Burdett Ginn, 1991)
- Chalkboard

Prior Knowledge and Experiences

- Students know the pattern sequence of odd and even in the number sequence.
- Students can identify eighth and quarter notes.

Procedures

1. Write the pattern "ti-ti ta" on the chalkboard. Ask the students to "pat-pat snap" this pattern several times.

2. Ask the students to examine the song "Billy Boy" and count the number of times the "ti-ti ta" pattern is repeated at the beginning of the song (six times). Write the pattern six times in a horizontal sequence. Have the students perform the song by saying "ti-ti ta" and using the "pat-pat snap" movement.

3. Ask students to use lower-case letters—*a* for "ti-ti" and *b* for "ta"— to describe this pattern (ab ab ab ab ab ab). Ask students how many items are in each of the six sets on the board (two).

4. Ask students to look for other places in the notation where the two eighth notes/quarter note pattern appears. Sing the song while following the notation and looking at the rhythmic patterns. (A small ensemble of rhythm instruments could play an ostinato while others sing.)

5. Tell students that mathematics is also filled with interesting patterns, and that they can solve problems with numbers and with musical notation by looking for patterns. Ask students to think of a place in the number line where this same "ab" pattern occurs (odd and even numbers). Ask students to determine whether the math pattern ends after six repetitions. (No, it continues to infinity.)

6. Invite students to recite the series of numbers from one to ten. Snap on the odd numbers and pat on the even numbers. Ask how this is similar to the notation pattern at the beginning of "Billy Boy" (both have every other item the same: "ti-ti ta" and "odd/even").

7. Ask students to illustrate this pattern sequence using objects, lines, or shapes. Then ask them to create and perform another rhythm that shows the "ab" pattern.

Indicators of Success

- Students locate or create, label and move to simple "ab" rhythm patterns. Students identify other "ab" patterns in mathematics. For example, when counting by fives, every other number ends in a five.

Follow-up

- Have students look at the notation of familiar songs in their student texts. Ask them to find, identify, and perform any repeated rhythm or melody patterns they find (some may be longer than two beats).

- Have students look for and describe repeated patterns in visual art works or posters in the music room or throughout the school.

STANDARD 9A

Understanding music in relation to history and culture: Students identify by genre or style aural examples of music from various historical periods and cultures.

Objective

- Students will aurally identify and discuss the Russian balalaika.

Materials

- "Minka," in *The Music Connection,* Grade 6 (Parsippany, NJ: Silver Burdett Ginn, 1995); *Share the Music,* "Songs to Sing and Read" (New York: Macmillan/McGraw-Hill, 1995); *Music and You,* Grade 3 (New York: Macmillan/ McGraw-Hill, 1991); or *World of Music,* Grade 6 (Parsippany, NJ: Silver Burdett Ginn, 1991), with accompanying CD and explanatory materials
- CD player
- Picture or photograph of a balalaika if one is not available in student texts
- Chorded zithers (such as Autoharps or ChromAharps) and small rubber mallets

Prior Knowledge and Experiences

- Students have learned about stringed instruments in American folk culture: the Autoharp/ChromAharp, guitar, banjo, and dulcimer, as well as the string family of the orchestra.

Procedures

1. Have the students work in small groups to name the stringed instruments they know. Invite them to share their lists with the class. Tell them that in addition to these, there is a stringed instrument from Russia called the "balalaika." Draw the students' attention to a photograph of the balalaika and ask them to describe what they see.

2. Play the recording of "Minka." Ask the students to listen for the sound of the balalaika in the accompaniment. As the students learn the song, share information about Russian culture and the use and history of this instrument.

3. Have the students create a sound similar to that of the balalaika by lightly and rapidly strumming rubber mallets on the strings of an Autoharp/ChromAharp while another student presses the appropriate chord bars to accompany "Minka" or another Russian folk song.

4. Invite students to share what they have learned about the balalaika and Russian culture by swapping facts with a partner. Then sing "Minka" to close the lesson.

Indicators of Success

- Students aurally identify the balalaika in the "Minka" recording.
- Student exchange information about Russian culture or the balalaika with a partner.

Follow-up

- Explore the sounds of stringed instruments in the music of other cultures. Possible instruments to explore are the koto (Japan), erhu (China), sitar (India), and banjo (United States).

STANDARD 9B

Understanding music in relation to history and culture: Students describe in simple terms how elements of music are used in music examples from various cultures of the world.

Objective

- Students will listen to recordings of Plains pow-wow music and will play various accent patterns on drums.

Materials

- "Chief Mountain," from *Pow-wow Highway Songs,* performed by the Black Lodge Singers (SOAR 125-CD, available from Sound of America Records, PO Box 8606, Albuquerque, NM 87198; telephone 505-268-6110)
- CD player
- Large pow-wow drums or bass drums
- Mallets/beaters
- Chalkboard

Prior Knowledge and Experiences

- Students have knowledge of syllabic accents in words.
- Students have basic knowledge of Native American regalia and customs.

Procedures

1. Open the lesson by writing the word "digest" on the board. Ask the students to pronounce the word and tell what it means. Explain that the placement of the accent determines the meaning and the way the word is pronounced (for example, DI-gest and di-GEST).

2. Write the numbers one to eight on the chalkboard and have the students clap eight beats. Then practice different accent combinations by having students select numbers to be accented and circling those numbers on the board. Have the students clap the accented patterns, play them on instruments, and move by stepping all eight counts and clapping on the accented beats.

3. Divide the students into groups of five to eight and have them sit around large drums, pow-wow style. (If you do not have enough drums, other students can be movers/dancers; have students switch roles during the lesson.) Show the students a picture of Native American drummers/singers sitting this way. Tell students that "drum" refers to the entire group around each drum. Explain that a pow-wow is an Indian festival with dance contests, food, and crafts. Attend one as a field trip, if possible.

4. Play the pattern 1̲ 2 3̲ 4 5̲ (accenting the underlined beats). Have students count the number of beats and then determine which beats were accented. Invite them to play the pattern. Have the students move by stepping on all counts and clapping on the accents. Then challenge students to clap on all counts and step on the accents.

5. Have each group (or one person from each group) choose accented beats using 1 2 3 4 5 to play for the class. Have other groups listen to the patterns and determine which beats are accented.

6. Explain that 1̲ 2 3̲ 4 5̲ is a pattern that occurs during traditional pow-wow drumming. If the last accent is very strong, it signals the end of the song. (*Note: The music often continues after these patterns; they are **not** ostinatos or a meter of five.*) Ask students to play steady beats with no accents and then to insert the five-beat pattern. Have students continue playing at a signal you give while someone else dances or improvises on a gourd rattle. To signal the end of the piece, make the last beat very loud.

7. Ask students to play the other five-beat ending patterns: <u>1</u> 2 <u>3</u> <u>4</u> <u>5</u> and <u>1 2 3 4 5</u>. Have students identify the accented beats, and have some of them move to the music.

8. Have students listen to examples of these patterns, such as "Chief Mountain" from the *Pow-wow* recording. Challenge them to identify the accent pattern at the end of each composition.

Indicators of Success

- Students demonstrate beat competency and one of the accented patterns played during the lesson.

- Students can describe how accents are used in these examples of Native American music.

- Students can describe some of the events or characteristics of a pow-wow.

Follow-up

- Have students listen to other examples of Native American music, including dance music from various recent pow-wow recordings by Native American musicians.

- Organize an all-school or grade-level pow-wow.

- Attend a pow-wow.

- Share the book *A Trip to a Pow-wow* by Richard Red Hawk (Newcastle, CA: Sierra Oaks Publishing Company, 1988).

STANDARD 9C

Understanding music in relation to history and culture: Students identify various uses of music in their daily experiences and describe characteristics that make certain music suitable for each use.

Objective

- Students will predict the style and describe the function of music in television advertising.

Materials

- Audio recording of a variety of excerpts from television commercials that use music
- Transcript of these commercials
- Audio-playback equipment
- Videocassette recorder and monitor
- Camcorder and blank tape

Prior Knowledge and Experiences

- Several days prior to this lesson students have determined their favorite television commercials that use music.

Procedures

1. Ask the students to brainstorm reasons why advertisers might use music in television commercials. Ask students to describe the music that accompanies their favorite commercials.

2. Play examples of commercials with the sound turned off. Recite the narration from the commercial while viewing the image with no sound. Ask the students what the music would add to the video image and narration. Ask the students to predict the kind of music that would go with this product. List adjectives they use to describe their choices.

3. Play examples with the sound turned on. Help students determine whether their predictions were correct. Have them list adjectives that describe the music that was actually used by the advertisers. Ask them to describe what the music added to the viewers' image of the product.

4. Invite students to work in small groups to create their own commercials. They will create their own product or service, write and edit a script, select or create accompanying music, practice their presentation, and perform it for the class. Videotape the final presentations and ask the class to critique the commercials, pointing out the strengths and making suggestions for improvements.

Indicators of Success

- Students design creative advertisements using appropriate music.
- Students use precise and descriptive language, including correct musical terms, when critiquing their classmates' work.

Follow-up

- Ask students to inform the class about the meaningful use of music in other places in their daily lives such as movies, instructional videos, or radio advertisements.

STANDARD 9D

Understanding music in relation to history and culture: Students identify and describe roles of musicians in various music settings and cultures.

Objective

- Students will observe and describe the role of the African master drummer.

Materials

- Videotape showing an African master drummer, from *The JVC Video Anthology of World Music and Dance* (Washington, DC: Smithsonian/Folkways, 1989); or the video library of a music text series
- Videocassette recorder and monitor
- Several sets of three notecards, each card having a different fact about an African master drummer

Prior Knowledge and Experiences

- Students have located Nigeria, Senegal, and Ghana on a map of Africa and are familiar with the drums used in African music as well as in American bands and orchestras.

Procedures

1. Invite students to form groups of three and have them list occasions when they have seen American drummers performing. Have them discuss whether these people are playing the drums for their life's work. Then ask students to name as many kinds of drums as they can. Show examples using pictures, photographs, or actual instruments when possible.

2. Tell the class that in many African tribes one of the most important people in any village or community is the master drummer. With the students still in groups of three, give each group a set of three cards with one fact on each card:

   • The master drummer learns the rhythm patterns from an older master drummer.

   • The master drummer is the leader of the music and dancing for the village.

   • The master drummer often plays one difficult pattern with one hand and a different pattern with the other hand.

   After each student has read the sentence on his or her card to the other group members, have the students discuss briefly how an African master drummer is different from other drummers they have seen.

3. Invite the class to watch a brief video segment showing an African master drummer. While the students are watching, encourage them to think about the information they have just learned.

4. After sharing the information on the cards and watching the video, ask the students to share words or phrases that describe the life and work of the African master drummer.

Indicators of Success

- Students accurately describe the dedication, talent, and responsibility needed to fulfill the position of an African master drummer.

Follow-up

- Invite students to create simple rhythm patterns and perform with a recording or video of an African percussion ensemble.
- Explore the roles of drummers in other musical styles and cultures, such as the tabla of India, taiko of Japan, the drum of Native American pow-wows, or the drummer in a jazz or rock band.

STANDARD 9E

Understanding music in relation to history and culture: Students demonstrate audience behavior appropriate for the context and style of music performed.

Objective

- Students will describe and demonstrate audience behavior appropriate to two styles of music.

Materials

- Audio-recorded examples of a traditional string quartet and a bluegrass, mariachi, or folk ensemble
- Audio-playback equipment
- Live performances of the same styles

Prior Knowledge and Experiences

- Students have listened to recordings and/or live performances of different styles and genres of music.

Procedures

1. Play an excerpt of a string quartet. Ask students to brainstorm where they might hear this music in a live concert and what kind of audience behaviors would be expected. List the answers on the board.

2. Play an excerpt of a bluegrass, mariachi, or folk ensemble. Ask students to brainstorm where they might hear this music in a live concert and what kind of audience behaviors would be expected here. List the answers on the board. Compare the two sets of answers and discuss the similarities and differences between them. Discuss why the two answers may be different.

3. Invite a string quartet from a high school, college, or community orchestra to present a short performance for the class. Study one of the pieces to be performed ahead of time. Practice audience behaviors appropriate to this style of music.

4. Invite a bluegrass, mariachi, or folk ensemble from a high school, college, or community group to present a short performance for the class. Study one of the pieces to be performed ahead of time. Discuss audience behaviors appropriate to the style of music.

5. After students have attended both performances, ask them to describe how the music and audience behaviors they experienced were similar to or different from what they had expected.

Indicators of Success

- Students exhibit appropriate audience behaviors at each performance.
- Students discuss why certain behaviors are appropriate in certain situations and inappropriate in others.

Follow-up

- Invite musicians from other styles and cultures to share with students the way an audience would respond to a live performance of their music. As the musicians perform, guide students in responding to the music in the appropriate fashion.

RESOURCES

Sources of Songs Used in This Text

Adzinyah, Abraham Kobena, Dumisani Maraire, and Judith Cook Tucker. *Let Your Voice Be Heard.* Danbury, CT: World Music Press, 1986.

Bradford, Louise L. *Sing It Yourself.* Sherman Oaks, CA: Alfred Publishing Company, Inc., 1978.

Choksy, Lois, and David Brummitt. *120 Singing Games and Dances for Elementary Schools.* Englewood Cliffs, NJ: Prentice-Hall, 1987.

Erdei, Peter and Katalin Komlos. *150 American Folk Songs to Sing, Read, and Play.* New York: Boosey and Hawkes, 1974.

Locke, Eleanor G., ed. *Sail Away: 155 American Folk Songs to Sing, Read, and Play.* New York: Boosey and Hawkes, 1989.

Johnston, Richard. *Folk Songs North America Sings.* Toronto: Caveat Music Publishers, 1984.

Jump Right In! The Music Curriculum. Chicago: GIA Publications, 1990.

Kersey, Robert E., compiler. *Just Five.* Miami, FL: Belwin-Mills, 1972.

Music and You, Grades K–8. New York: Macmillan/McGraw-Hill, 1991.

The Music Connection, Grades K–8. Parsippany, NJ: Silver Burdett Ginn, 1995.

Share the Music, Grades K–6. New York: Macmillan/McGraw-Hill, 1995.

World of Music, Grades K–8. Parsippany, NJ: Silver Burdett Ginn, 1991.

Listening Selections Used in This Text

Bach, Johann Sebastian. "Jesu, Joy of Man's Desiring" (chorale).

Beethoven, Ludwig van. Second Movement of Symphony no. 7.

Billings, William. "Chester" (chorale).

Bizet, Georges. "Carillon," from *L'Arlésienne Suite no. 1.*

Brahms, Johannes. "Hungarian Dance no. 6."

"Chief Mountain," from *Pow-wow Highway Songs.* Performed by the Black Lodge Singers. SOAR 125-CD. Available from Sound of America Records, PO Box 8606, Albuquerque, NM 87198; telephone 505-268-6110.

Chopin, Frédéric. Prelude in A.

Copland, Aaron. "Circus Music," from *The Red Pony Suite.*

Dvorák, Antonín. "Largo," from Symphony no. 9 ("From the New World").

Ellington, Duke. "Dooji-Wooji."

Froseth, James, and Phyllis S. Weikart. "Latin Rock," from *Music for Movement*. GIA Publications MLR 187.

Grieg, Edvard. "In the Hall of the Mountain King," from *Peer Gynt Suite no. 1*.

Grieg, Edvard. "Norwegian Dance no. 2."

Handel, George Frideric. "Minuet," from *Music for the Royal Fireworks*.

Haydn, Franz Joseph. Second Movement of Symphony no. 94 in G Major ("Surprise").

Holst, Gustav. "Mars," from *The Planets*.

Kabalevsky, Dmitri. "Gallop" and "March," from *The Comedians*.

Kodály, Zoltán. "The Viennese Musical Clock," from *The Háry János Suite*.

Mahler, Gustav. Third Movement of Symphony no. 1.

"Makoce Wakan," from *Red Thunder*. Canyon Records ETR 7916. Available from Canyon Records and Indian Arts, 4143 North 16th Street, Phoenix, AZ 85016; telephone 602-266-4823.

Maraire, Dumisani. "Mai Nozipo," from *Pieces of Africa*. Performed by the Kronos Quartet. Elektra/Nonesuch 979275-2.

Marais, Marin. *The Bells of St. Geneviève*.

Mozart, Wolfgang Amadeus. "Minuet and Trio," from Symphony no. 39.

Mussorgsky, Modest. "Ballet of the Unhatched Chicks," from *Pictures at an Exhibition*.

Orff, Carl. "O Fortuna" and "Tanz," from *Carmina Burana*.

Peter, Paul, and Mary. "Boa Constrictor," from *Peter, Paul, and Mommy*. Warner Brothers 1785.

Prokofiev, Sergei. "Departure," from *Winter Bonfire Suite*.

Prokofiev, Sergei. "Troika," from *Lieutenant Kijé Suite*.

Rodgers, Richard, and Oscar Hammerstein II. "Getting to Know You," from *For Our Children*. Performed by James Taylor. Disney 60616-2.

Saint-Saëns, Camille. "The Swan," from *Carnival of the Animals*.

Stravinsky, Igor. "Berceuse," from *Firebird Suite*.

Tchaikovsky, Piotr Illyich. "Dance of the Sugar Plum Fairy," from *The Nutcracker Suite*.

Winter, Paul, Paul Halley, and Oscar Castro-Neves. "Kurski Funk," from *Earth Beat*. Performed by the Paul Winter Consort. Living Music Records LD0015.

Additional Resources

Abramson, Robert. *Rhythm Games.* New York: Movement Press, 1973.

* Anderson, William M., and Patricia Shehan Campbell, eds. *Multicultural Perspectives in Music Education.* Reston, VA: Music Educators National Conference, 1989.

Benward, Bruce, and David B. Williams. *DoReMi* computer program. Bellevue, WA: Temporal Acuity Products, 1992.

Brennan, Elizabeth Villarreal. *The Singing Wind: Five Melodies from Ecuador.* Danbury, CT: World Music Press, 1988.

Brocklehurst, Brian. *Pentatonic Song Book.* New York: Schott, 1976.

Burton, Bryan. *Moving within the Circle.* Danbury, CT: World Music Press, 1993.

Campbell, Patricia Shehan. *Lessons from the World.* New York: Schirmer Books, 1991.

Campbell, Patricia Shehan, Ellen McCullough-Brabson, and Judith Cook Tucker. *Roots and Branches.* Danbury, CT: World Music Press, 1994.

* Carder, Polly, ed. *The Eclectic Curriculum in American Music Education.* Reston, VA: Music Educators National Conference, 1991.

Choksy, Lois. (1981). *The Kodály Context.* Englewood Cliffs, NJ: Prentice-Hall, 1981.

Choksy, Lois. *The Kodály Method.* 2d ed. Englewood Cliffs, NJ: Prentice-Hall, 1988.

Choksy, Lois, Robert M. Abramson, Avon E. Gillespie, and David Woods. *Teaching Music in the Twentieth Century.* Englewood Cliffs, NJ: Prentice-Hall, 1986.

East, Helen. *The Singing Sack: 28 Song-Stories from around the World.* London: A&C Black, 1989.

Ellis, Karen. *Domino: Selected Songs from the Virgin Islands.* Nazareth, PA: Guavaberry Press, 1990.

Finckel, Edwin A. *Now We'll Make the Rafters Ring: 100 Traditional and Contemporary Rounds for Everyone.* Pennington, NJ: A Cappella Books, 1993.

Findlay, Elsa. *Rhythm and Movement: Applications of Dalcroze Eurhythmics.* Evanston, IL: Summy-Birchard, 1971.

Fowke, Edith. *Ring around the Moon.* Englewood Cliffs, NJ: Prentice-Hall, 1977.

Fowke, Edith. *Sally Go Round the Sun.* New York: Doubleday, 1969.

Frazee, Jane. *Discovering Orff: A Curriculum for Music Teachers.* New York: Schott, 1987.

Hackett, Patricia. *The Melody Book.* 2d ed. Englewood Cliffs, NJ: Prentice-Hall, 1992.

Hackett, James W. *The Zen Haiku and Other Zen Poems of J. W. Hackett.* Toyko: Japan Publications, 1983. (Distributed in the U.S. by Zen View Distributors, PO Box 313, La Honda, CA 94020-0313.)

Han, Kou-Huang, and Patricia Shehan Campbell. *The Lion's Roar: Chinese Luogu Percussion Ensembles.* Danbury, CT: World Music Press, 1992.

Jaques-Dalcroze, Emile. *Rhythm, Music and Education.* Trans. H. F. Rubenstein. London: The Dalcroze Society, 1970.

Jessup, Lynn. *World Music: A Source Book for Teaching.* Danbury, CT: World Music Press, 1992.

The JVC Video Anthology of World Music and Dance. Washington, DC: Smithsonian/Folkways, 1989.

* Kaplan, Phyllis R., and Stauffer, Sandra L. *Cooperative Learning in Music.* Reston, VA: Music Educators National Conference, 1994.

Keetman, Gunild. *Elementaria: First Acquaintance with Orff-Schulwerk.* London: Schott, 1970.

Lomax, Alan. *The Folk Songs of North America.* New York: Doubleday, 1960.

Martin, Bill. *Listen to the Rain.* New York: Henry Holt, 1988.

Mead, Virginia. *Dalcroze Eurhythmics in Today's Music Classrooms.* New York: Schott, 1994.

Nguyen, Thuyet Phong, and Patricia Shehan Campbell. *From Rice Paddies and Temple Yards: Traditional Music of Vietnam.* Danbury, CT: World Music Press, 1992.

Orff, Carl, and Gunild Keetman. *Orff-Schulwerk: Music for Children,* 5 vols. English adaptation by Doreen Hall and Arnold Walter. Mainz, Germany: B Schott's Sohne, 1956.

Phillips, Kenneth H. *Teaching Kids to Sing.* New York: Schirmer Books, 1992.

Red Hawk, Richard. *A Trip to a Pow-wow.* Newcastle, CA: Sierra Oaks Publishing Company, 1988.

Sam, Sam-Ang, and Patricia Shehan Campbell. *Silent Temples, Songful Hearts: Traditional Music of Cambodia.* Danbury, CT: World Music Press, 1992.

Seeger, Ruth C. *American Folk Songs for Children.* New York: Doubleday, 1948.

Steen, Arvida. *Exploring Orff.* New York: Schott, 1992.

Szonyi, Erzsebet. *Musical Reading and Writing,* 3 vols. New York: Boosey and Hawkes, 1974–79.

Titon, Jeff T., ed. *Worlds of Music.* 2d ed. New York: Schirmer, 1992.

Vanaver, Bill. *Sheaves of Grain: Songs of the Seasons from around the World.* Danbury, CT: World Music Press, 1990.

Warner, Brigette. *Orff-Schulwerk: Applications for the Classroom.* Englewood Cliffs, NJ: Prentice-Hall, 1991.

Weikart, Phyllis S. *Teaching Movement and Dance,* 2 vols. Ypsilanti, MI: High Scope, 1982.

* Wiggins, Jackie. *Composition in the Classroom: A Tool for Teaching.* Reston, VA: Music Educators National Conference, 1990.

Winner, Ellen, Lyle Davidson, and Larry Scripp, eds. *Arts Propel: A Handbook for Music.* Cambridge, MA: Harvard Project Zero and Educational Testing Service, 1992.

*Available from MENC

MENC Resources on Music and Arts Education Standards

Implementing the Arts Education Standards. Set of five brochures: "What School Boards Can Do," "What School Administrators Can Do," "What State Education Agencies Can Do," "What Parents Can Do," "What the Arts Community Can Do." 1994. #4022. Each brochure is also available in packs of 20.

Music for a Sound Education: A Tool Kit for Implementing the Standards. 1994. #1600.

National Standards for Arts Education: What Every Young American Should Know and Be Able to Do in the Arts. 1994. #1605.

Opportunity-to-Learn Standards for Music Instruction: Grades PreK–12. 1994. #1619.

Perspectives on Implementation: Arts Education Standards for America's Students. 1994. #1622.

Prekindergarten Music Education Standards. Brochure. 1995. #4015 (set of 10).

The School Music Program—A New Vision: The K–12 National Standards, PreK Standards, and What They Mean to Music Educators. 1994. #1618.

Teaching Examples: Ideas for Music Educators. 1994. #1620.

The Vision for Arts Education in the 21st Century. 1994. #1617.

MENC's *Strategies for Teaching* Series

Strategies for Teaching Prekindergarten Music, compiled and edited by Wendy L. Sims. #1644.

Strategies for Teaching K–4 General Music, compiled and edited by Sandra L. Stauffer and Jennifer Davidson. #1645.

Strategies for Teaching Middle-Level General Music, compiled and edited by June M. Hinckley and Suzanne M. Shull. #1646.

Strategies for Teaching High School General Music, compiled and edited by Keith P. Thompson and Gloria J. Kiester. #1647.

Strategies for Teaching Elementary and Middle-Level Chorus, compiled and edited by Ann Roberts Small and Judy Bowers. #1648.

Strategies for Teaching High School Chorus, compiled and edited by Randal Swiggum. #1649.

Strategies for Teaching Strings and Orchestra, compiled and edited by Dorothy A. Straub, Louis Bergonzi, and Anne C. Witt. #1652.

Strategies for Teaching Middle-Level and High School Keyboard, compiled and edited by Martha F. Hilley and Tommie Pardue. #1655.

Strategies for Teaching Beginning and Intermediate Band, compiled and edited by Edward J. Kvet and Janet M. Tweed. #1650.

Strategies for Teaching High School Band, compiled and edited by Edward J. Kvet and John E. Williamson. #1651.

Strategies for Teaching Specialized Ensembles, compiled and edited by Robert A. Cutietta. #1653.

Strategies for Teaching Middle-Level and High School Guitar, compiled and edited by William E. Purse, James L. Jordan, and Nancy Marsters. #1654.

Strategies for Teaching: Guide for Music Methods Classes, compiled and edited by Louis O. Hall with Nancy R. Boone, John Grashel, and Rosemary C. Watkins. #1656.

For more information on these and other MENC publications, write to or call MENC Publications Sales, 1806 Robert Fulton Drive, Reston, VA 22091-4348; 800-828-0229.